Remembering

Xinxiang

William L. Adams

NORTEX  Austin, Texas

FIRST EDITION
Copyright © 2001
By William L. Adams
Manufactured in the U.S.A.
By Nortex Press
A Division of Sunbelt Media, Inc.
Austin, Texas
ALL RIGHTS RESERVED.

ISBN   1-57168-654-1

To
Hu Rui-juan
"Helen"

And in life's autumn
A second daughter
A precious gift
Adored
Always

Contents

Preface

My fascination with China began twenty years ago when, upon the completion of a long teaching stint in Australia and the Solomon Islands, my wife and I decided to take a week's vacation in Hong Kong enroute back to the States. Although we were not able to make a foray into Mainland China at that time as we had hoped—entry visas then being more difficult and time consuming to obtain—Hong Kong itself was sufficiently "Chinese" to hook me on China and its people. How curious it all was. Roaming the back streets of Kowloon, turning each corner, I was constantly being surprised by new visions of beauty, squalor, or, more often than not, some beguiling blend of both. Before that week was out, my appetite had been thoroughly whetted, and I knew I just had to return for more. Though not so my wife. Having grown accustomed to the easy grace and insouciance of the Solomons' black natives, she found, by contrast, the Hong Kong Chinese to be cold, hard-faced, grasping and, yes, inscrutable. She felt uncomfortable in their presence. And so, when nearly twenty years later, I was given the opportunity to spend a sabbatical year in China, she was less than enthusiastic about the prospect.

How quickly that initial impression of hers evaporated once we arrived in what we since have come to regard as "the real China," interior China, and especially that most populous of all Chinese provinces, with its 100 million-plus people the absolute demographic and historic core of China, Henan. What wonderful people it has: so intelligent, so industrious, so unspoiled, and so affectionate. How poignantly we will miss them.

But that is not to say Roselyn and I have become uncritical admirers of China. We like the Chinese as a people, but all is not well in China. There is corruption in this land—deep-rooted, pervasive corruption. And China, at least for the present, is hardly a friend of America or the West. This is a country that criticizes and denigrates America and intentionally distorts American motives and actions at every turn—in its newspapers, in its news broadcasts and in its school textbooks. It is a country that refused to denounce Saddam Hussein's invasion of Kuwait and abstained from taking any side in the Persian Gulf War. This is a country that offered moral support to Slobodan Milosevic in his efforts to ethnically cleanse Kosovo. This is a country that baldly lies to its own people and tells them that the Taiwanese are eager to be absorbed into the People's Republic and are only frustrated from doing so by Taiwan's unrepresentative government. This is a country that denies its people access to CNN, and does all it can to obstruct its own people in their struggle to gain an unbiased, valid picture of the outside world. And this, too, is a country that still exalts in displaying its tanks, missiles and military might in stupendous, Stalinesque-style parades. In short, China remains a dangerous nation.

Fortunately, there is hope. The "Opening Up" and "Four Modernizations" Policies set in motion by Deng Xiaoping are bearing fruit and may in time produce a peaceful, prosperous and democratic China and not simply a powerful China. That presumably is the goal of America's "carrot and stick" China policy (wherein the carrot is usually offered by Democrats while the stick is wielded by Republicans), and this policy may go some way in driving the Chinese "mule" in the desired direction. But it must be remembered that mules are stubborn and the Chinese mule is huge. It will likely remain a contrary brute and go pretty much where it pleases.

But this book is not an academic work, and only touches sparingly and indirectly on political and economic issues. This book is much less ambitious. It is only my account of what is was like to live, teach and travel in "the real China" at the turn of the millenium. There is great beauty and happiness to be found in "the real China," and great ugliness and sadness as well. What I have seen of these I've recorded here.

I have a number of people to thank. At the University of Texas at Brownsville several people played a part in getting me to China and sustaining me while there. These include History Chairman Jim Sullivan, Liberal Arts Dean Farhat Iftekharuddin, Provost Ray

Rodriguez, President Juliet Garcia and friend and colleague Tony Knopp and his wife Alma. At Henan Normal University in Xinxiang I am indebted to English Department Vice-Dean Li Wenzhong and colleagues Lu Yuefeng and Wang Yun. My *waiban*, the ever competent, ever kind Mr. Li Quifa, helped in all the affairs of daily life from pay to plumbing, mail to meals, and offered advice and friendship too. I thank our friend Krishna Singh for his help and companionship throughout our stay in China and for being part of our little "family" while there. And then there's our "Helen" (Hu Rui-juan), an absolute delight of a girl who began as our guide and interpreter and ended as our daughter. She brought us so much joy that forever "Helen" and "happiness" will be synonymous in our memories. It is to Helen that this book is dedicated.

In helping to prepare this book for publication I thank Patti Vela who entered the text on computer discs. Brownsville's foremost artist, Don Breeden, with the assistance of commercial artist Frank Valdez, has rendered a superb cover based upon an idea and Xinxiang photograph supplied by my wife. My friend and patron Dr. Bennie Walthall, a retired Arabian-American Oil Corporation geologist, kindly funded this project, just as he has done with my previous books.

Indeed, deepest gratitude goes to my dear wife Roselyn. I thank her for accompanying me to China, bearing up with me in our cramped apartment, entertaining my students four nights a week so that they could practice their oral English skills, helping me to grade student essays and diaries, and banging out this book's manuscript on a forty-year-old manual typewriter with more quirks than could be counted. Well done.

And finally I would be remiss if I failed to mention the contribution made to our stay in China by the U.S. Consulate at the American Embassy in Beijing—particularly the Visa Unit and American Citizens Services Unit. I found you folks to be so consistently incompetent, so unfailingly rude, so supremely arrogant, so utterly unhelpful in every matter, large or small, that I thought you should know it, and others should too. You are a disgrace to America.

Willam L. Adams
Tioman Island, Malaysia
July, 2000

Prescript

Tioman Island, Malaysia—July, 1999

I'm floating. I'm good at floating. It's something the navy taught me. When your ship goes down, don't panic. And don't strike out for some unseen distant shore. You'll never make it. Better to just lay back in the water, relax if you can, and wait for someone to come get you.

So now I'm floating, drifting about, wafted by the gentle swells. Actually, I'm in no danger. In fact that's my wife Roselyn there on the shore sunning herself in the beach chair. The guy she's talking to is "Crazy Dave." Crazy Dave's the Indian manager of this Malaysian resort—the "Swiss Cottages." Kind of an incongruous name really for this rundown clump of tin-roofed shacks sitting amidst the palm trees on this equatorial island. Legend has it the cottages were a sort of bolt-from-the-blue inspiration of some entrepreneurial genius who'd just read of the Swiss Family Robinson's delightful ordeal of having been marooned on a jungle island. But however that might have been, it all must have taken place a very long time ago. The cottages have suffered decades of neglect, and the resort, seedy and forlorn, sits off on its own in a clearing, largely unnoticed by the tourists who rumble by in the shuttle bus that runs between the island airstrip and the big, Western-owned vacation mecca further along the coast road where fatso Anglo-Saxons

1

with belly packs ride about in golf carts and occasionally waddle down to the beach and stand splay footed looking out to sea.

But Roselyn and I enjoy the cottages and we enjoy Dave, "Tiger Man" he likes to call himself, cause he likes to drink Tiger-brand beer. He likes to drink it a lot. Dave suits the place to a "T." He's also a bit seedy and forlorn but not without charm. He pads about the place barefoot and half-naked in a droopy pair of purple shorts. He's lean, dark and raffish with a gold front tooth, gold ear-rings and piratical looks. Thirty-eight and single, his ever-alert eyes frequently scan the beach for stray females. In between times he manages the place, although "manage" may be too grand a description for the function he performs. His employees—his "boys," Kemal, Camille, Ali and the others—are also his drinking buddies, and can quickly turn sassy with Dave if he drives them too hard. For maybe an hour or two in mid-morning when Dave emerges bedraggled and hungover from his cottage he'll carry out the official duties of his day. He'll wave his arms around a bit, remind the boys, "I'm boss. You've got to do what I say," and coax them to drag off a few fallen palm fronds, rake the sand a bit, and chop a little firewood for the evening barbecue. All these chores are performed half-heartedly while the boys keep one eye cocked on Dave. After an hour or so, Dave will crack the first Tiger or two and his supervisory powers start to wane. Soon the boys' energy wanes too. They prop their rakes against palm trunks and ease on over to join Dave for a Tiger. Now the day gets back on track and Dave and the boys work themselves up into a party mood by dusk when they'll fire up the barbecue and roast some chicken and mutton on skewers. Afterwards they settle into cards and really serious drinking and keep going till an hour or two before dawn. Another day on Tioman is done.

Today Dave's looking especially rocky. He's got blood-red eyes and a big gap where his solid gold tooth fell out of its socket during an especially heavy bout three nights ago. He doesn't know where that tooth could be. He's tapped into his foggy memory to reconstruct the evening as best he can and retraced his probable steps a dozen times. Zero. He's also given the boys orders to keep their eyes peeled when raking, but so far nothing's turned up. So now Dave's got a suspicion that he may have unknowingly washed the damn thing down his throat with a quaff of Tiger. To cover that possibility he hasn't used a regular toilet in three days. Instead, he spreads a newspaper out on his bedroom floor, dumps his load, and then dissects the stools with a knife. But so far no luck, and, as I say, it's been three days. The thought's occurred to him that the tooth might have got stuck in a loop or fold of his intestine and so every little bit, whenever he thinks about it, he jumps up and down and violently writhes his abdomen about trying to dislodge it. It's an inconvenience.

This morning I watched him trooping miserably across the clearing towards his cottage with his rolled up newspaper in hand and shouted out to him, "Good luck, Dave!" to buck up his spirits, but all he returned to me was a despairing sort of half wave. His door was closed for a long time while he was in there doing his sad business, his slicing and dicing. When he emerged to stand on his cottage step you could tell immediately from the set of his shoulders that once again he'd failed to find much of value. Poor Dave. This whole tooth business has been rather tedious for him.

Still, I guess we've all got our own problems, and I'm no exception. You know what I'm thinking about mostly while I'm floating here? I'm thinking that our month on this island is almost up and in a few days my wife and I will be flying into central China. I'm a little worried about this. I have the TV images fresh in my mind of the anti-NATO and anti-American demonstrations in Beijing following the "May 8th Incident" in Yugoslavia wherein U.S. smart bombs were mistakenly targeted on China's Belgrade embassy, killing three Chinese journalists within the building. The Chinese government chose to regard the bombing as intentional and ratcheted the affair into an international incident, complete with orchestrated student protest marches which culminated in daily peltings of the U.S. Embassy in Beijing with rocks, bricks, and paint bombs. I can still see images of our timid embassy staff members peek-a-booing out from behind curtains and corners while ranks of fierce-eyed Chinese students swept down the tree-lined street outside. The fallout of the incident was sufficiently strong to delay my Chinese work visa and to prompt my colleagues into advising me against going to China for safety reasons.

Nevertheless, I've determined to go—we've determined to go—and I hope I haven't made a mistake; I hope this isn't foolhardy. I've made it a joke with my friends and colleagues that Roselyn and I won't mind being roughed up a bit and spat upon as long as they don't cause us actual permanent bodily harm, but, in fact, that is exactly what I'm most worried about. I don't have an ounce of masochism in me, and being knocked about has no appeal to me whatsoever. And who knows what the reaction to two Americans will be like in the center of China. International journalists were present to cover the demonstrations in Beijing, Shanghai, Hong Kong and the other easily accessible cities on the Chinese periphery, but where we will be going in central China—Xinxiang—we will be invisible to the prying eyes of international journalists, and remote from any protection which might be afforded by embassy or consular walls. We will be on our own.

I'm floating.

Arriving

We lift off from Shanghai at midday. Within a minute or two Hongqiao Airport and the squalid ranks of gritty gray-brown tenements that form the giant city's western fringe begin to be obscured by clouds and the rust-colored smog. Our fellow passengers—all Chinese—are not sophisticated, experienced travellers. They do not lounge with newspapers or nap from boredom (whether real or shammed) like jaded Westerners. No, these sons and daughters of the People's Republic draw a collective gasp at the moment of take-off. As we rise, every porthole, *every* porthole, of this China Southern Airways' Boeing frames one or two heads as passengers *en masse* unhitch their seat belts, disregard flight attendants' orders, and crane necks to see what they can before the clouds close in. Awed silence gives way to excited chatter as fingers point out landmarks and neighborhoods to one another, and as we thunder up through the white fluffy world of the clouds there are delighted "oohs" and "aahs." The thought occurs to me that I may come to like these unpretentious people.

Our plane is aimed west and slightly north towards the provincial capital of Zhengzhou, 500 miles inland. Flying over China is not like flying over other nations. Screened though it is by a nearly solid cloud mass reminiscent of an Antarctic plateau, one senses the weight and power of the nation hunkered below just as one would sense a living, breathing animal—a very large, living, breathing animal—in a pitch-black room. China has true *gravitas:* the size of it, the antiquity of it, the humanity it contains, the suffering it has endured. Fly over Canada, Belgium, Australia, fly over almost any nation in the world, and if you're not a native of that country, what do you feel? Nothing, right? I know of only a very few lands that generate nearly universal palpable emotion similar to China's. A number of non-American air travellers, some of whom were not even admirers of America, have remarked to me that flying over the United States produces an unexpected emotional rush similar to that which is reported by Christians descending towards the Holy Land and Moslems towards Mecca. Such is the evocative power of a name, and "China" has it.

Now and then in the 90-minute flight rips in the cloud cover reveal the landscape below, the great Central China Plain bounded by the Yellow and Yangtze Rivers, the most densely inhabited and intensely farmed region on earth—the "rice bowl" that sustains one-fifth of mankind. But even knowing this does not prepare you for the intensity of the spectacle: the marvelously green fields, the seemingly numberless villages, the wonderful intricacy of the irrigated rice fields stretching from horizon to horizon. The sun's shafts dance over these flooded, earthen-walled paddies illuminating each in turn like facets of a jewel. The scene has the effect of making you, in some way, proud to be human. Man has done some great things, built mighty bridges, dams and cities, but in my eyes nothing rivals the achievement of "The Plain" that the Chinese have created and tilled over the course of several millennia and which represents the life's labor and legacy of literally billions of peasants.

When we land at Zhengzhou there are only four other planes on the ground. This as much as anything gives you a hint of the relative lack of development in the Chinese interior. Zhengzhou has three million people and is the political and commercial capital of Henan, the most populous of China's 22 provinces and five autonomous regions—a province with 103 million people, millions of more people than California, Texas, New York and *Canada* combined, all jammed into an area smaller than Oklahoma. You'd expect Zhengzhou to have a huge airport something on the lines of Chicago's O'Hare, but no, just four planes and a handful of gates.

And that's because Henan is an economic backwater, one of China's poorest regions. All the boom and bustle of the "New China" Westerners have been hearing about is largely confined to Beijing and the nation's coastal regions, especially such entrepôts as Dalian, Tianjin, Shanghai, Ningbo, Guangzhou, Shenzhen and, of course, Hong Kong.

Some political commentators and futurists, including Rober Kaplan and Hamish McRae, go so far as to predict that the relatively wealthy coastal regions (and believe me this is only *relatively* speaking—no Westerner could possibly regard *any* region of China as wealthy) will eventually break away from the terribly impoverished interior. I do not myself think this at all likely. China is not a hodgepodge of nationalities like the former Soviet Union; it is one of the most ancient and homogenous societies on earth: Han Chinese make up 92 percent of the population. Moreover, the government is frightfully jealous of maintaining its territorial integrity. It will keep all of its lands and incorporate Taiwan as its twenty-third province sooner or later. But the prediction does serve to underline the huge disparity in economic fortunes between Beijing and the coastal entrepôts (the only cities most Western tourists and businessmen come to know when they visit China) and the far more vast, largely agriculturally-oriented, and still pitifully poor interior.

We are met by a fresh-faced youth of 24, Xiao Li, who serves as an official driver for Henan Normal University which has me on loan from the University of Texas at Brownsville for a year to teach English Writing and British and American History. Xiao Li is to use the school's black Santana Volkswagon to drive me and my wife Roselyn, and our six pieces of luggage, two hours north to the city of Xinxiang (Shin-she-ang) where the university is located. Xiao Li formerly served as a chauffeur in the People's Liberation Army and he is a superb driver, which is very fortunate because no where have I seen such difficult driving conditions as we now encounter—not in New York City, not in Rome, not even in Mexico. The difficulty comes not so much from the density of the traffic on the road, but from the variety of the traffic. There are still very few privately-owned cars on the road in China, especially interior China, but there is everything else: buses, trucks, tractors, trishaws, motorcycles, horses, horses and carts, man-pulled carts, and bicycles, bicycles, bicycles. Leaving the airport, the highway is for the most part theoretically four lanes, a *non-divided* four lanes, but aside from a general understanding that northbound traffic should sort of tend to stay in the right-hand lanes . . . sometimes . . . and southbound vehicles should tend to stay in the left-hand lanes quite a bit, there are no rules. We all just go like bats out of hell. The object of course is somehow to thrust your way through the tangled mass of vehicles and always, always get ahead of whoever's in front of you. Anything goes: pass on the shoulders, pass by whipping into the lanes of the oncoming traffic, create a new lane by pounding, pounding, pounding on your horn then hold the horn down in a steady blare and somehow squeeze between that bus on your left-hand and that crazy cartload of hay on your right. Zig between those two trishaws; there'll be an easy four inches of clearance between their wheels and yours. Go for it! Look out! What's that up ahead? A man stands in the middle of the road with his arms outstretched. Behind him there's a truck with a dent in its side, a smashed motorcycle, and a man laying in the road with his leg at a weird angle. A woman kneels beside him. The traffic parts to either side of this mini-tragedy and races on. Momentarily stymied by a horse wagon in front of us and trucks to our sides, motorcycles, bikes and trishaws zip past us. Drawing abreast and then slowly pulling ahead of us is a trishaw powered by a polio victim with legs no bigger than a baby's, but this man has rigged himself a chest-high sprocket and chain and "pedals" it with his massive arms. A child rides in the trishaw's metal cargo box. The child stares through the window at us foreigners and smiles.

After two hours of this, we leave the main highway and turn off onto a two-lane road that in a short while brings us to the outskirts of Xinxiang.

Xinxiang

Xinxiang, which ironically translates as "New Town," is situated in one of the earliest settled regions of China, or, for that matter, the world. Two hundred miles southwest of Xinxiang where the Wei tributary joins the Yellow River, and near the base of that latter river's so-called "Great Loop," Chinese civilization first emerged 5000 years ago. Both the world's first known instrument of worked iron, "The Sword of China," and the most ancient "oracle bones," Chinese characters inscribed on ox bones and tortoise shells, were unearthed within a fifty-mile radius of Xinxiang.

Today Xinxiang has a population of 700,000 and ranks as the fifth largest city in Henan Province. The city serves as the principal market for the fertile farmlands in the northern portion of Henan Province, those counties north of the Yellow River. The city follows the typical Chinese town planning scheme in use since ancient times wherein a strict grid is created by aligning streets north-south to intersect with east-west streets at right angles, creating blocks. Aside from serving the surrounding agricultural region's needs, the city has important coal seams nearby and tunnels honeycomb the substrata. Numerous pitheads dot the neighboring countryside. The city has over 200 factories including textile mills, a television assembly factory, a tractor factory and China's largest refrigerator plant (Frestech). Factory workers typically earn between 500–700 yuan per month (U.S. $60–78), and receive deeply subsidized housing for which they only have to pay U.S. $1-2 token rent. The city is also a major rail center as the nation's principal north-south rail artery (Beijing-Wuhan-Guangzhou) intersects at Xinxiang with an important east-west line with terminuses on the coast.

By no stretch of the imagination could Xinxiang be considered a beautiful city. It has far too may imperfections for that. There is for instance the matter of its filth. Like all Chinese cities it is filthy. And we're not talking about ordinary filth, the kind of filth that could be easily tidied up by clearing away the rubble from construction sites (which here tends to be shovelled or bulldozed into heaps to the sides of the new buildings and just left) or carting off the piles of garbage—rotting vegetables, broken flip-flops, shattered glass, rags, bloated rat carcasses, discarded bike tires and unidentifiable crud—that seems to fill up every ditch, depression and vacant lot in the city. No, here we are talking about truly serious squalor. Ancient filth. The kind of filth that makes you reluctant to touch any doorknob, any stair railing, or God forbid, to enter any public toilet. It's the kind of filth that requires you to take off your shoes and put on the house slippers that are kept at every home's entryway lest you track in what you've been trodding upon out on the streets and sidewalks: urine, human feces, and the tubercular phlegm which slickens pavements throughout the city. The Chinese do not employ handkerchiefs and are constantly hacking, spitting and clearing their clogged nasal passages by depressing one nostril with a finger and blowing the contents of the other onto the sidewalk or floor. Toddlers wear trousers that have the entire crotch and bottom area cut our of them so they can squat and urinate or defecate whenever and wherever they get the urge.

Nor is it just the germs and other human contaminants that spoil the city's environment. There is a general grittiness and dustiness about the city. Being in a coal mining region, trucks, trains and carts constantly roll through the city and inevitably leave behind a detritus of coal dust, and the city's power comes from coal-fired thermal electric plants. The city's garbage is burned, not buried. Belching brick smokestacks punctuate the urban landscape and have, over the decades, lent every older building in the city a grit-gray patina. Indeed, gray is your overall impression of the city. And rather than attempting to combat this general grayness the city long ago bowed to the inevitable and in the spirit of "if you can't lick 'em, join 'em" adopted gray as the principal motif in building construction. Pre-revolutionary buildings were often made from slate-gray bricks, while Maoist era structures—mainly densely sited five- and six-story apartment blocks—were usually erected in raw concrete, left unpainted, and quickly degenerated to the point where today whole swaths of the city look like and, indeed, are slums.

More recently, in the Nineties, a number of ten-, twenty- and even thirty-story highrises have gone up (mainly banks and commercial towers), and these have the futuristic flare Asian architects seem to favor. But even here something always seems to just miss. Despite the often bold, undeniably striking exteriors, funds tend to run out before the interior appointments can be properly completed. You'll have this spanking new edifice and then the interior will be finished out with cheap secondhand office furniture and, in some cases, proper flooring will be lacking: no rugs nor tiling, just a bare concrete floor. Another solution resorted to is to concentrate resources on the building's ground floor, the one the public will most often see, and then scrimp on everything above ground level.

The dustiness of the city is owing to the texture of the region's soil. The soil type is known as loess. Loess is light brown in color and extremely finely granulated. Compress a clod of loess in your palm and it disintegrates into talcum powder-like dust. It is this dust diluted by water that gives the Yellow River its tint and is eventually spewed out of the river's coastal estuaries to stain the Yellow Sea. Even a slight breeze will serve to lift exposed loess granules from the farm fields surrounding Xinxiang and many of these granules will be deposited on the city. The powder finds its way through any window crack, any door jamb, creating a housewife's nightmare. No furniture surface can be kept free of it for even a single hour. But more importantly, this nearly invisible powder is in every breath of air Xinxiang residents draw, and it is only partially filtered by nostril hairs. This accounts in large measure for the constant hacking, coughing and sneezing of the locals.

Another unappealing aspect of Xinxiang is that it has an appalling smell about it. That fact prompted a previous visiting professor to Xinxiang's Henan Normal University to cut short his appointment, return to the United States and write a scathing article for a national monthly bluntly entitled "China Stinks." Well, frankly, Xinxiang does stink. The smell of ordure is omnipresent. It's worse at some times than others, especially in the mornings, but it is always perceptible. The smell even permeates one's clothes. The source of the odor is human waste. Many of the city's older homes and apartment blocks are not connected to the sewage system and just have cesspools. These cesspools are emptied by an army of laborers equipped, not with trucks and suction hoses, but with nothing more than buckets, scoops, metal drums and horse-drawn carts. You see a steady stream of these carts clip-clopping through the streets bearing their evil cargoes to the farm fields on the city's outskirts where the "honey-pots" will be sold for fertilizer. This fertilizer is spread on the fields North, East, South and West of the city insuring that in whichever direction the wind is blowing, the stink will waft over the city.

Incidentally, the pariahs who make their living scooping and hauling this human waste seem to have a peculiar sort of dignity about themselves. As their clip-clop heralds their arrival in a street and the crowds of pedestrians melt away before them, ducking this way and that with hands cupped over noses and mouths, they will be sitting in their rags atop their loathsome carts with heads held high, inured to the reek, and will disdainfully flick their whips at their ponies' haunches. If your eyes should meet theirs, they'll stare you down every time.

Perhaps by now you are getting the impression that Xinxiang is virtually unlivable, that its poverty, its gritty grayness, its dirt and dustiness, its smell, would make life there unbearable. Well that impression would be wrong. It might surprise you, but despite the city's numerous and undeniable imperfections, it is still quite livable, and, in many respects, even quite pleasant. Lives *are* being lived here, and, for the most part, those lives are good lives.

Xinxiang has many saving graces. Foremost of these is the basic decency of the people, and, after all, it is people who make up a city, and set its tone. There is a deep-grained civility about these people that the ancient culture has instilled over the millennia. Not even the harshness of the revolution and the Maoist years could eradicate the Chinese people's nearly innate politeness, their desire to avoid giving offense. This quality informs their every action, and, in so doing, brightens every day and lightens every life. This spirit, this atmosphere of good will, suffuses Xinxiang.

Nor is the city lacking more tangible charms. It has many lovely parks, both large and small, that you often stumble upon in the most unlikely corners—little islands of serenity. There are the countless little sidewalk shops and street stalls that sell almost any product from books to dried bats or offer any service from instant clothing or shoe repair to fortune telling or palm reading. There are open-air markets that can be found almost anywhere, springing up literally overnight as farm families come convoying into town in their horse-drawn wagons and set out their wares: produce in baskets, chickens in cages, piglets on leashes. And, best of all, there are the city's dozens of beautiful tree-lined avenues.

I like the city best just at dusk when the pace of the city slackens and the residents—couples, families, friends—are strolling the streets, lazily pedaling bicycles, gathering at the sidewalk eateries, usually consisting of not much more than three or four plastic tables with chairs and a brazier, that serve snacks, tea and beer at miniscule prices that even the poorest can afford. As the evening approaches, these gregarious people sit in groups talking, playing cards, playing mah-jong, socializing. At those times if you are sitting with your wife, sipping beer and look down the avenue's canopy of birch trees and Chinese elms shading the strollers, cyclists and clip-clopping horse carts from the last shafts of the setting sun, you'll be content. Content to be in this poor man's Paris. Content to be in Xinxiang.

The Chinese

Aside from a smattering of Tibetans, Manchus and Mongols, the Chinese population is comprised of Han Chinese (92 percent). The Han vary somewhat in size with those in the northern half of the nation typically being two to three inches taller and proportionately heavier than their southern brethren. Most Americans are more familiar with the smaller, southern members of the Han because ever since Chinese immigration to America began in the mid-1800s the immigrants have come mainly from the southern and southeastern provinces.

Xinxiang residents belong to the larger, northern variety of Chinese and as such are not much shorter than most Europeans or Americans—although they are lighter. This is probably a reflection of their leaner diet and harder, more physically demanding lives. You could stand alongside any busy Xinxiang street watching the flow of pedestrians and cyclists and you'd be hard pressed to spot more than three or four overweight persons in an hour, and you'd almost never see a truly obese person such as those that lumber through stateside malls. No, the overwhelming majority of Chinese are nicely built with lean, lean bodies. Most of the women retain lithe, willowy bodies into their fifties, while most men remain fit and wiry even into old age. This is quite evident because farmers and laborers of all ages often work barechested in the warmer months.

Overall, I think you'd have to consider the Chinese an attractive race. Some people would argue that such qualitative judgments on racial beauty are inappropriate, if not impossible, but if we are honest with ourselves we know distinctions do exist. Just as everyone knows that gazelles and tigers have intrinsic beauty, so we know that warthogs and hippopotamuses do not. Likewise, if you can't see that there is a huge difference between the Malays, probably the most exquisite of all races, and the unfortunate Australian Aboriginals then you either lack aesthetic taste of are intentionally being blind.

And though the Chinese are not as attractive a group as the Malays, they are still quite attractive. They have the physical assets of their fine bodies, their straight, jet-black hair and their unusually high cheekbones. Opinion varies concerning their narrow eyes. Some non-Asians do not like them, finding them inscrutable or even sinister looking like the slit eyes of a snake or cat, while others admire their almond shape and the dashing upward slant towards the temples. Exotically beautiful. Personally I like their eyes and find the Chinese attractive—especially the women. They can be quite nifty.

Of course not all Chinese are physically favored. The Chinese do not have nearly as broad a spectrum of appearances as Caucasians (after all, Chinese have only the one hair color—black, and only the one iris color—dark brown) but they do exceed Caucasians in their variety of head shapes, and some of these shapes are rather unfortunate. Quite a number of Chinese have a chubby, perfectly globular head and when such a soccer ball is placed atop the normally lean, angular physique it is incongruent and, frankly, a little silly looking. Still other unfortunates, considerable numbers of them, suffer a V-shaped head of an acuity almost never seen in other races. These individuals have a head remarkably broad between the temples with exceptionally wide set eyes, but the cheeks and jawbone drastically taper to a very narrow, pointed chin, leaving very little space for the mouth which is often no bigger than a quarter, and the sharp teeth can be seen working in the orifice. Not nice to look at and not nice, I'm sure, for those persons who have to bear the burden of such a head. If you saw "The Last Emperor" you might recall the actor who portrayed one of Emperor Puyi's vicious prison interrogators. That actor shared the affliction.

Of course of more consequence than physical appearance are the mental attributes of the Chinese. They are an intelligent people. There is even some empirical evidence that they might be the most intelligent of all peoples. At least, this was suggested by Richard J. Hernstein and Charles Murray's study on human intelligence, *The Bell Curve* (1994). Although this book sparked a firestorm of academic and political criticism because it reported a huge disparity in Black and White IQ averages (Black Africans 70–85; African-Americans 85–86; Europeans and European-Americans 101–102) and the two authors were sometimes dismissed as White racists, what became overlooked in the controversy was that Hernstein and Murray found not whites but East Asians (the Chinese, Japanese and Koreans) to have the highest overall intelligence of the earth's people, with an average IQ of 104–105.

But regardless of the credence one chooses to give the Hernstein-Murray study and the relevance and validity of IQ scoring in general, surely the marked success of the millions of Chinese who have found themselves living and competing in foreign societies speaks well of their mental agility. Almost anywhere you go in Southeast Asia and the Pacific region you encounter "Overseas Chinese" who have established themselves as a successful minority which frequently forms the commercial class within the host nation. Indeed, so successful have the Overseas Chinese been, sometimes they are referred to as "the Jews of Asia" and, historically, like the Jews, they have sometimes been persecuted as the scapegoats of choice by the jealous, less successful native inhabitants. Recall, for instance, their victimization during the Malay "Emergency" of the 1950s; their expulsion and flight from South Vietnam as the "Chinese Boat People" following the 1975 communist takeover; and the bloodbath they were subjected to in Indonesia in 1965 when an estimated half million of them were slain.

In America, too, the Chinese have proven their mettle. Not only do Chinese-American youths (along with the other East Asians) routinely drub every other ethnic minority and White Americans on S.A.T. scores and other measures of academic success, but Chinese-Americans as a whole have proven themselves to be a "Model Minority." Whatever index one chooses to apply—educational attainment, family income, family cohesiveness, welfare dependency rate, prison incarceration rate—Chinese-Americans have compiled an enviable record in America.

The history of China also testifies to the intelligence of the Chinese people. It should not be forgotten that China's Yellow River Valley was one of the four original sites of world civilization (along with Mesopotamia and the Nile and Indus Valleys) where the benefits of a settled agricultural system, urbanization and government organization were first discovered and applied. And, moreover, of those four original civilizations, China has been the only one which has succeeded in maintaining its civilization, its culture, in anything like and unbroken chain over the vicissitudes of five millennia. That, in itself, bespeaks of the intelligence, vigour and durability of the Chinese people, especially when it is considered that during many of those fifty centuries Chinese civilization was the most advanced in the world. The Middle Kingdom's cities were the largest and wealthiest on the planet, and its scholar/administrator civil servants were the most efficient and honest. This was the civilization that invented paper, the printing press, the compass and gunpowder.

Of course it can be counterpoised that had China's civilization been so superior, it would have been the Chinese rather than the Europeans who explored the world and imposed a cultural hegemony. Well, unarguably, by the time the first Portuguese ships arrived in the Sixteenth Century, Chinese civilization had grown complacent and ossified. But the long, sad chapter of an enfeebled China's decline and foreign domination has ended. There truly is a resurgent China, and one has only to look at the wealth and energy of the Chinese societies of Taiwan, Hong Kong and Singapore to gain a hint of the huge motherland's potential.

Nor should purely anecdotal evidence of Chinese intelligence be dismissed. Speak to Westerners who have lived amongst the Chinese, and you'll find most all agree the Chinese are very smart. Such opinions should have weight particularly in light of the fact that the foreigners who have been engaged to work and live in China are rarely your typical man-in-the-street. As a group they are highly educated and well travelled. Frequently they are familiar with a host of nations and societies. If they say the Chinese are bright, you may take it that they know something of what they are talking about.

Just as any reasonably intelligent individual can quickly gauge the intelligence of persons whom they see in everyday life and work, so those living amongst the Chinese will soon come to appreciate their mental quickness. It can be inferred from many small observations that quickly mount up: a truck breaks down at the side of the road almost anywhere, anytime, and a host of adept hands emerge to fix it; the Chinese avocation of reading—young and old, rich and poor, standing in doorways, sitting on curbs, riding in hay carts, book or newspaper in hand, the profusion of bookstores; the people's nearly universal love of games, complex, cerebral games: cards, chess and mah-jong—lunch break at construction sites and sweaty laborers bunch around chess boards; the less than universal but still broad appreciation of good art, literature, music and architecture. And finally, how could anyone have witnessed China's stupendous 1999 Fiftieth Anniversary parade in Tiananmen, a perfectly executed parade with 500,000 participants, by far the greatest parade staged anywhere, anytime, and doubt the brains, taste and organizational skills of the people who conducted it?

Even the Chinese language is illustrative of Chinese intelligence—who but they could have mastered it? The characters are, of course, lovely to look at—as pleasing to the eye as the French language is to the ear and just as indicative of keen aesthetic taste—but, unfortunately, the written language has little relation to the spoken language as is the case with alphabetically– based languages. Thus, the Chinese, in mastering their native language, are, in fact, mastering two languages, both of which are complex and difficult. For this reason, U.S. government agencies (such as the Central Intelligence Agency, the Foreign Service, and the various military branches) which oversee foreign language training programs rate Chinese as a "Class Four" language, a tiny category that includes the world's three most difficult languages: Chinese and its two offshoots, Korean and Japanese. Nor is Chinese only difficult for foreigners; it is difficult for the Chinese themselves. For this reason one of the communist reforms introduced in the 1950s was the program to substitute simplified *jiantizi* characters for the traditional *fantizi* characters (reducing the number of pen strokes comprising characters from 20 or more to a maximum of twelve). This effort helped boost the national literacy rate (which is construed as the ability to read a minimum of 2,000 characters) to its current high of

82 percent, but that still leaves 18 percent (220 million people) beyond the literate pale.

The official spoken language, Mandarin, or Standard Chinese, is also a rascal. Slight inflections of pitch called "tones" given to many identical, or nearly identical, words produce an array of widely diverse meanings. A comparison would be the spoken "too" (to, too, two) in English, except for the fact that almost every spoken word in Chinese has multiple meanings, meanings which can only be inferred from the context of the sentence or detecting nuances in inflection or "tone." Hence, *"qing wen"* is "excuse me" or "please kiss me," while, more dangerously, *"gei wo shui jiao,"* "give me boiled dumplings," could easily be mistaken for *"gen wo shui jiao,"* "sleep with me."

Enunciating the correct "tones" for the largely monosyllabic language also calls for frequent intensity of expression, with the result that the spoken language is harsh, abrupt, even angry sounding. Non-Chinese speaking newcomers to the country overhearing the Chinese in conversation often fear a fight is about to erupt . . . until the conversation terminates in smiles and backslaps.

Perhaps the greatest attribute of the Chinese as a people is the deeply civil nature of the society they have constructed. From the time one awakens and swings his feet out of bed in the morning until one tucks himself under his quilt at night, I would think the Chinese suffer less from the tensions of everyday living, less from the frictions of interpersonal relations than almost any people on earth. To what this satisfying state of affairs is owed is difficult to pinpoint but surely must be partially attributed to a nearly instinctual understanding of the necessity for personal tolerance in an historically crowded society, plus remarkably broad adherence to ancient Confucist principles regarding "correct action" in all interpersonal relationships. Nor should the contribution of socialist precepts stressing communal obligations be overlooked here. One of the few positive legacies of China's Communist "Dark Age" was that the Chinese Communist Party was not just paying lip service to Marxist ideals of human equality. The Party *did* insist that dignity be paid the common man—the worker of the field, the worker of the factory.

So how exactly does all this goodwill play out in everyday life? Well, it means, for instance, if you are a suited businessman bargaining in the market with a raggedy peasant with a trishaw-load of lettuce that you won't be calling each other "comrade" these days, but then neither will anyone be calling the other "sir." There will be a relaxed civility between the two and a regard for each other's respective roles in society. There will not be, as in most other societies, the subtle tension of trying to exactly calibrate the precise balance of arrogance-deference that is "seemly" in the exchange. How many such minute human interchanges go to making up a typical mortal's day? Fifty? A hundred? Well, if you could subtract from your day—by a hundred fold—the tension inherent in assessing just what degree of deference you should demand or obeisance you must render in these human mini-confrontations, your life would be a lot more relaxed and a lot more sociable. When you hop into a cab alone you'll ride in the front alongside the driver and not in the back like some chauffeured nabob. And, of course, you won't be tipping that driver. Tips are shunned everywhere in China, quite firmly refused. (The exception is Westernized, tip-hungry Hong Kong where everyone from hotel doormen to bank tellers with their tip bowls are as aggressively grasping as New York panhandlers.)

And speaking of panhandlers, they are another unwholesome segment of most other societies largely absent in China. Despite pervasive poverty, especially in the Chinese interior, beggars are rarely seen. And when they are encountered, almost always they will be old people—old people apparently without families to care for them or old people who have been abandoned by their families. These unhappy creatures may sometimes be seen in their rags and wretchedness dragging themselves through public parks or along commercial thoroughfares, or working the crowds outside bus depots, train stations or tourist spots. They may occasionally accost you at your table in outdoor cafes and eateries. Some of them are in a stage of grottiness that is truly awful to behold. Rags bound round their feet with twine. Shreds of blankets draped across their shoulders for shawls. Matted hair uncombed for months hanging in uncouth ropes. Nine out of ten locals will contemptuosly wave these nuisances off, but a pittance garnered here and there from the other ten percent evidently sustains these unfortunates. Of course in the really big cities like Beijing and Shanghai foreigners provide the beggars with a more lucrative target, but in Xinxiang and most other interior cities foreigners are too rare to be a factor in any beggar's maintenance.

Probably the biggest reason for the scarcity of beggars in China is the importance the Chinese place on "saving face"—preserving one's dignity at almost any cost. Most Chinese would rather starve than subject themselves to the disgrace of begging for a livelihood. The Chinese are a proud people, proud even in their poverty. They will take great pains to treat others with respect (and, consequently, the Chinese are notorious flatterers), but they expect to be treated with similar respect in return. To correct, criticize or remonstrate with a Chinese privately, or, more seriously, in public or before his family, is a grave insult to his "face." A flippant gesture, a thoughtless display of contempt, may be repaid with a lifetime of enmity.

The ultimate in "losing face" in China is forcing someone to bend his knees. The Chinese of olden times may have been reduced to kow-towing before their superiors, but modern Chinese abhor doing so to *anyone* today. The most serious punishment parents can mete out to their children is not striking them, but demanding that they assume a kneeling position on the floor before them—and staying there for ten minutes, an hour, half a day. Tears of shame and humiliation will roll down the child's face and the lesson will be burned into the child's psyche for a lifetime.

I myself became sensitive to the bended knee posture when one of my college students visited my apartment along with her parents. During the course of the visit the girl casually knelt on the carpet beside my chair while showing me a passage in her textbook. A day or so later the girl told me that her parents had been shocked and ashamed to see their daughter on bended knees—and before a foreigner no less!

In like vein, I remember an incident in 1999 when the governor of Henan hosted a convocation and banquet for all the "foreign experts" in his province (about 100 Russians, Brits, Americans, French, Germans, and Japanese) to thank us for our services. The event was held in Zhengzhou's lavish, four-star, Western-managed Sofitel Hotel and early arrivees, including our small Xinxiang contingent, were conducted to a sumptuous lounge/waiting area where we were served with tea. To our astonishment, and the angry dismay of our Chinese guides and interpreters, the lovely lounge hostesses, wearing traditional Chinese gowns and bearing teapots, had been trained to drop to their knees several paces from guests' chairs and to creep forward on their knees to fill our teacups. Shameful! Against every principle—including women's equality—New China stands for.

Once one can grasp the importance the Chinese place on their "face," one can begin to appreciate the value they place on human life—and value it they do. This comes as a surprise to some Westerners. Many Westerners believe that Asians in general and the Chinese in particular regard human life as cheap. This delusion stems in part from the Western capitalist mindset whereby any commodity's value is determined by the principle of supply and demand: whenever and wherever there is an overabundance of a commodity (in this instance human life) its value must inevitably decline. So in the teeming Asia of the Western imagination—the Asia of the "yellow hordes"—it is difficult to understand how life can have much value. After all, it was these same Asians, these Chinese, who regarded life so cheaply during the Korean War that they could afford to wear down American defensive lines by using "human wave" tactics—recklessly squandering Chinese soldiers' lives in relentless frontal assaults until the G.I. defenders literally ran out of ammunition and were engulfed by subsequent "waves" and the "Yellow Tide" swept on. How could such people place much store on human life? Hence, some Americans' puzzlement over the more recent "May 8th Incident." That 1999 tragic, mistaken bombing by an American plane of the Chinese Embassy in Belgrade cost the lives of three Chinese and caused massive, anti-American, anti-NATO demonstrations across China, including one at my own campus. Now let's overlook for the moment that China's communist government cynically and deliberately misrepresented the incident and incited the demonstrations for domestic political purposes and just look at the three lost lives. How, many Americans wondered, could the Chinese get so upset over three lives? China has a zillion people, so how could three lives more or less possibly matter to them? Well, the fact is, three lives *do* matter to the Chinese. The Chinese government knew this when they made the decision to manipulate the incident for their own purposes. The fact that the Chinese people do have such a high regard for human life guaranteed that the government could successfully "fan" the fires of outrage. Make no mistake, a bereaved Chinese mother will wail just as loudly for her dead child as will any mother anywhere. Maybe louder. Why do I say louder? Well, remember most Chinese are atheists and they have not even the slight consolation of religion and the hope, the possible prospect, of the loved one's soul surviving in an afterlife. For most Chinese a life gone is a life gone—forever and irrevocably. Add to this fact the Chinese emphasis on family over the individual and the wrenching away of a life is even more traumatic than it is in Western societies where individualism is stressed over family and the roots between an individual and his family and community are shallower.

Indeed, the close-knit nature of Chinese family life is almost beyond the comprehension of modern-day Westerners, certainly the Westerners of North America and northern Europe where the fabric of family life has been unravelling over the course of several generations. For a U.S. citizen to witness the silken bonds that tie a Chinese family together will evoke a nostalgia for a rural America of the long ago past.

My perspective on Chinese family life comes to me largely second-hand through conversations with my students (almost all of whom are females) and readings of their essays and daily diaries. These students, overwhelmingly the children of peasants, sincerely pine for their families and villages. Homesickness is a serious problem at the university and afflicts nearly every student. Letters and telephone calling cards partially abate the problem, but in serious cases, students have to ask their tutor's permission to return to their villages for a short while in mid-semester. Most often it is attachment to their mothers that calls them home since Chinese fathers typically preserve a somewhat remote position in the family and seldom demonstrate their affection. Of course, these students are also drawn by the concept of "family" as a whole, and in rural China this generally means an extended family: mother and father, minor children, unmarried adult daughters, adult sons and their wives and children, and finally, various aged relatives. The attachment of a daughter to a family is tenuous compared to the permanent bond of a son, especially an eldest son, since a daughter is, as the idiom goes, a "basin of water" to be "poured out" in time to her eventual husband's family.

But home these students do go. You'll see the tell-tale signs building in their diary entries: the worrying about their hard-working parents in the fields at radish-digging time or peanut-pulling time, the wondering about what their "naughty" little brother is doing, the sleepless nights in their dorm, the sudden bouts of crying. Then, the next thing you know, the classroom monitor reports to you that Miss Hu or Miss Wang or Miss Zhiang got emergency leave and took the train home last night. A week later she'll be back in class sitting there body relaxed and face aglow and you'll read in her diary of the visit: showing up by surprise and embracing her parents amidst the corn rows, rolling dumplings for a family feast, crawling into bed with her mother at night, holding her leathery hand, whisperings till dawn beneath the quilts. How lovely.

Of course not every aspect of tight-knit Chinese family life is altogether positive. For one thing, children, especially children of the interior provinces, face an enormous dilemma when they complete their educations. Nearly all parents want their children to return to the immediate vicinity of the family—or, at the very least, the nearest sizable town or city—and pursue their careers there, and assist the family financially. However, it is not usually in the interior provinces that career prospects are the brightest for young people, and, anyhow, many youths have begun to feel the lure of the big coastal cities, particularly Shanghai and Guangzhou (Sodom and Gomorrah to Chinese parents). Many a young person faces the anguishing choice of pursuing their own dream or bowing to filial duty.

Another unpleasant truth about Chinese families is that many of them are not happy ones. Divorce is still quite rare in China, especially interior China, but of course many married couples are miserable, trapped in loveless marriages and held there by bars of convention and intimidating public opinion. To divorce is to lose an enormous amount of "face." What often happens is that a peasant boy and girl will marry young, and then the boy will somehow manage to "rise" either through access to education, or by virtue of his own hard work and business acumen. Soon he will outpace his ignorant peasant wife whom he may come to despise. Frequently he will seek an alliance with a younger woman or a more accomplished woman. I can remember a very uncomfortable restaurant dinner my wife and I had with just such a Chinese couple—the husband being a professional acquaintance of mine. My wife and I and this man sat at one end of a dining table conversing while his peasant wife sat alone at the far end (where he had seated her) noisily gobbling her food. With a despairing voice my acquaintance remarked: "My wife was once beautiful." He stared at her. Gimlet eyes. Not a flicker of warmth. She might have been a bug.

One other facet of Chinese family life that deserves mention has to do with the impact of the government's "One-Child Policy." Most Westerners have at least heard of this experiment in population control, although the policy itself is often misunderstood. This policy, which aimed at first to slow and then to eventually halt Chinese population growth, was first proposed by Beijing University scholar Ma Yin Chu shortly after the communists came to power. The idea was brought to the attention of Chairman Mao, but due to the deterioration of Sino-Soviet relations and the very real threat of war in the 1950s and 60s the policy had to be postponed. Instead, the Maoist axiom of "The more people, the more power" held sway, and no checks were placed on the burgeoning population. However, once foreign relations improved and the Cultural Revolution had run its course, in the late 1970s Deng Xiaoping finally moved to implement the policy. He was acutely aware of China's population time bomb and the very negative impacts unfettered population growth was having with regards to China's limited food resources, its urban explosion, its housing shortage and its overall economic prospects. Unless the population growth rate could be kept below the economic growth rate, per capita incomes and living standards could not improve. Accordingly, in 1979 the government put into effect a number of measures to assuage the situation. For one thing, the legal marrying age was raised from 20 to 25—so China would have to cope with only four generations of people, rather than five, over the next 100 years. That would provide the society with a little breathing room. (N.B.: In 1999 the legal marriage age was eased down to 24 for urban males, 22 for urban females and rural males, 20 for rural females. However, these younger couples are forbidden to conceive children until they are both over 25 years old.) But more importantly, in 1979 the "One-Child Policy" also went into effect and was to remain in effect for 70 years, with a terminating date in 2049. The policy is breathtaking in scope and will, if it is successfully imposed, not only eventually cap population growth, but even lead to negative population growth for a time.

But what is often misunderstood is that the "One-Child Policy" is no where near full implementation. It is only strictly imposed in urban areas and, even then, couples may elect to have more than one child if they are willing to pay the violation fine, which varies from 2000 to 6000 yuan ($240–$720) depending on province. That is not a negligible sum in China where per capita income averages $2800, but then neither is it insurmountable. Still, most urban couples abide by the policy, partly for economic reasons, partly for political reasons (and to protect one's career prospects), and partly because children are just plain inconvenient in metropolitan areas where apartments are small and living space is at a premium. As for rural areas, the "One-Child Policy" is just a name . . . a "dream" really. Peasants, who it is to be remembered make up 70 percent of China's population, are partially exempt from the policy. Peasant families feel they must have a boy—a boy to carry on the family's name and to provide "power"—sheer physical strength—to help work the family's farm which is usually unmechanized. Consequently, if a peasant couple gives birth to a daughter, or even daughters, the couple are allowed to "keep going," without penalty, until they have a son. However, should they persist and have a subsequent child once they *do* have a son, they are at the mercy of their village's communist leaders, who have a free hand in meting out draconian penalties, such as confiscating the family's tractor or even demolishing their home. But, all in all, the fact that population growth is slowing even in China's rural areas has more to do with economic factors, limited land resources and the farmer's own fear of having too many mouths to feed than it does with the population strictures imposed by the government.

But certainly the single-child family has become the mode in Chinese cities in the twenty-plus years since the policy went into effect. Xinxiang is no exception, and my married colleagues all have but a single child if, indeed, they have any at all. Visit any of them in their apartment and there you will find the freshly-scrubbed, nattily-dressed apple of the parents' eyes. He or she will have their own room, oodles of toys, and shelves of books and educational materials. Mommy and daddy will dote on them. And make no mistake, many Chinese worry about the effect this lavishment of love upon a single child is going to have on the personalities of the three generations of children the 70-year policy will produce. Will they all be brats? Already these offspring are referred to as "The Little Emperors" or "The Little Empresses" and many of them *are* spoiled. You can see it. You can watch them. Still, most of my colleagues with whom I've discussed the Little Emperor Syndrome—

it's a very popular topic in China—are optimistic that these children are being adequately disciplined and will be socially well-adjusted, ready to meet whatever demands their parents and society have in store for them.

One peculiarity of China that Westerners first notice when they come into the country, a peculiarity which derives from the tremendousness of the population and the densely-packed nature of the society, is that there isn't much privacy to be had. This is awkward for most Westerners and especially for Americans who are used to elbow room and who prize their privacy, but it doesn't seem to bother the locals in the least. Most Chinese grow up in extended families and most Chinese houses and apartments are very small. I guess people are just used to living on top of one another. My students, mainly girls, live eight to a small room, piled into four bunkbeds. They are as intimate as kittens, crawling over each other and bumping into each other all the time. On frigid nights in the heatless dorms they'll double or triple up in the beds to share their body heat. This kind of living I would find difficult, but they take it as a matter of course. I think they like it. When they come to visit us in our apartment they come in packs of eight or ten or even twenty and pile up on the couch or chairs. By sharing laps, eight might sit on the couch while two or three share each chair. They drape their arms over each other and are constantly fooling with each other's faces and hair. They seem to need to be in constant physical touch with another body. Sometimes this intimacy gets a little out of hand. When one of them sneezes, the other will be there with a tissue to tidy up the nose. Once during a test I watched when one of my girls sneezed and a wad of snot shot out of her nose onto the desk. Quick as a wink her deskmate wiped this up with the tips of her fingers and deposited it in a scrap of paper she tore from the corner of her own test paper. There were no words exchanged. It was so very quick, so very neat, so very natural. You wouldn't catch Westerners doing this.

The lack of privacy in Chinese toilets is also disconcerting to Westerners. Most public toilet facilities for both men and women are your "squat" toilets—we're talking here about a hole in the floor—and partitions are seldom provided. There are just rows of the damn things. People file in, squat down and do their business. In a men's room you'll find men squatting there bare-bottomed waiting for nature to take its course. They may be reading news-papers or chatting with their neighbors. Good grief!

The lack of privacy extends too to everyone knowing every-one else's business. Next to "How are you?" the most common Chinese greeting is "Where are you going?" followed up by "What will you be doing there?" There's really not much that's out of bounds when talking to the Chinese. Someone you've just met or, for that matter, haven't met and just happen to be standing next to in a line or on a bus is almost sure to want to know how old you are, how much money you make, what you paid for the shoes you're wearing. As likely as not a crowd will gather because others will want to get clued in too. If I'm out with Helen, my guide and in-terpreter, people, strangers, also need to know if we sleep together.

The fact is the Chinese are a very curious people. Anything dif-ferent, slightly out of the ordinary, is not only fascinating, but also fair game. Staring is not considered in the least rude. No one is going to avert their eyes from you if you're a cripple, a dwarf, or you've got two heads. And, of course, you, as a foreigner, fit in here too. You're free entertainment in a poor country. And if you are a foreigner located in the interior, far off the beaten path taken by tourists, you'll enjoy celebrity status. People will be gawking at you always and everywhere. If you're an exhibitionist craving attention, you'll be in heaven; if you're at all shy or reserved, you'll be in hell. From the moment you step out of your home in the morning until the time you close the door behind you at night, you're going to be stared at. Your every movement will be scrutinized. You'll have the power to stop a peasant dead in his tracks at ten paces. His mouth will drop open. If he is car-rying something, that's liable to drop too. If you smile and say *"ni hao"* ("hello"), he'll smile fit to burst and nod *"ni hao, ni hao, ni hao."* If you're out and about on your bike, you'll find farmers on carts whipping up their donkeys to draw abreast of you and cyclists ma-neuvering to maintain pace with you so they can study you for a awhile. If you're plowing your way afoot through teeming city side-walks every pair of eyes you meet is going to be locked on to your blue eyes. And the effect produced by those blue eyes is comparable to that which albino pink eyes used to have in the pre-contact lens era: fasci-nation and a tinge of fear. So very strange. Young children sometimes cry. One of my college students, for God's sake, asked me once: "How did you get eyes like that? What happened to them?"

A final important aspect of the Chinese I would like to mention concerns their morality. More than once in Xinxiang during public lectures I have been asked to comment on China's prospects for delevoping a First World-level economy. My response has been that I think China will develop a first-rate, First World economy *if* they can find a way to contain corruption. That is a big "if." I'm afraid they might not be able to do it, in which case they'll be just as surely mired in permanent Third World status as such other once promising economies—but moral morasses—as Mexico or Brazil. The scourge of corruption could defeat this nation just as it has so many others. And that would be such a shame because most of the people are honest and decent. They deserve success.

You witness the basic Chinese decency all about you. Aside from the hucksters operating at the few tourist haunts—Xi'an, the Great Wall, Hong Kong, anywhere in Hong Kong—the people aren't out to cheat you. In the markets, the shops, the restaurants and taxis you don't even have to bother counting your change. People who refuse tips are not people who are going to try to bamboozle you.

My wife and I began to appreciate Chinese honesty a week after we came to Xinxiang and my wife unwittingly left her purse, with a very hefty sum inside, at a department store counter—the counter for flashlights and small table lamps. The counter clerk chased all over the five-story building until she found us to return the purse. Such displays of human decency move me, as they do most of us, and after a few minutes' reflection I decided to return to this girl's counter and give her five percent of the purse's contents as a reward. I knew that five percent would probably represent more than a month's pay for her. But this girl, thin, unattractive, and with poverty written all over her, refused the money at once. I thought for a moment, then firmly laid the money on her counter and briskly walked away. Moments later she stood in her cheap, run-down shoes blocking me at the store exit. She opened my palm and placed the money inside.

Now I realize one isolated instance of honesty does not an honest nation make, but then this was not just an isolated instance. I have seen many such demonstrations of honesty in China, enough to convince me that it is real and pervasive, part of the culture, and a virtue parents instill in their children from the earliest age. My students often talk about this and write about this—how their parents hammered home the lesson to always be honest, always be truthful, regardless of the consequences.

Schools, at all levels, also reinforce the need for honesty and a virtuous life. At my university, as at other universities in China, "Personal Morality" is a required course. Where in America, in the West, would a *public* university *offer* such a course, let alone *require* such a course? Most of the course's content is about what you'd expect, but you might be surprised to learn that it also teaches the virtue of chastity prior to marriage. Chastity for Heaven's sake! How quaint! Or so it must seem to Americans and Northern Europeans where sex in any way, shape or form is glamorized, and the public schools revel in "getting down and dirty": teaching the nitty-gritty of sex techniques, the desirability of "alternative" sexual styles, and dole out condoms like candy to children who have barely broached puberty.

But premarital sex is a phenomenon my Chinese students remain refreshingly naïve about, or, on second thought, more serious about. I've spoken privately to a few of my senior students, students whom I know well and whose judgments I trust, and asked them to estimate how many of their *senior* classmates, aged 22–23, have engaged in sex. Their response is the same: virtually none of the seniors, male or female, have ever had sex, certainly not more than two or three percent. Moreover, some estimated that not more than ten percent of the seniors had even kissed someone of the opposite sex of their own age. (Interestingly, one of my senior girls I spoke with said none of these figures would apply to the males in the Physical Education Department who, as in universities virtually everywhere, have the reputation of being playboys: stupid and immoral, but able to attract girls of a certain type with their superb bodies.)

Certainly my students seem sexual innocents to me. Their diaries, both of the young men and women, are replete with romantic sentiments, their cravings for love, and often these will have a fantastical quality. But their hopes of finding, as they usually put it, an "excellent boy" or an "excellent girl" whom they might love "forever," is almost always seen as fated for the future, an event to be put off until after they have graduated and established themselves in a career. And this is the way university officials want it. The need to delay romance so that it doesn't interfere with studies is constantly driven home in peer "discussion groups" and forums held by administrators and the powerful class tutors. "Intimacy" between a boy and a girl, and here we mean holding hands, kissing and such, can result in the pair being "criticized," a serious matter, which can, in turn, result in a diminishment of the pair's scholarship stipends, scholastic opportunities and career prospects. Still, some romancing does go on and couples can be seen strolling around the campus at night, embracing in the shadows. Now and then a "drive" will be launched to curtail such behavior, but such actions are rarely completely successful. An "action" to segregate the sexes in the university's numerous cafeterias and canteens collapsed after only a few weeks. The action had been prompted when some couples were detected engaging in intimacies while dining: boys and girls using their own chopsticks to poke morsels and tasty tidbits into the mouths of their beloved.

But in any instance of actual sex between students, the administration moves vigorously and ruthlessly. In 1998 a girl student was impregnated by a senior boy shortly to graduate. A Xinxiang hospital reported the girl's condition to university officials who, in turn, tracked down the malefactor and expelled him—absolutely ruined him. But then, too, the girl had been ruined. And that's exactly the Chinese expression used to describe any girl who has been raped, seduced into having premarital sex, or given birth to a child out of wedlock: she has been "ruined." And the loss of "face" to the girl's parents and family is devastating. They are "ruined" too.

One might think if the Chinese are so honest and so strict regarding sexual mores, that they must be equally honest and strict in broader community matters. After all, if there is trust, restraint and fidelity in sexual and family matters, surely those virtues can be applied in civil matters as well. Sadly, however, that is really not the case. Once one leaves the preserve of the Chinese family home, there is an erosion of integrity and a concomitant rise in corruption. One of the most important reasons for this is the abiding principles of *Li Shang Wang Lai* or "*guanxi*" for short. *Guanxi* might loosely be translated as "You scratch my back, and I'll scratch yours." In other words, it is the age-old "payback" system. To get things done in China you depend on your *guanxi* network. Do you have a son needing placement in the workforce? Don't rely on his mediocre merits, but find a relative or acquaintance that can pull some strings, circumvent the hiring process, cut through the red tape, and get that boy hired. But, remember of course, you are now in someone's debt, and that debt is going to have to be repaid sometime, somehow. Whether you are a policeman, a teacher, a bureaucrat, you can be sure your benefactor will call upon you at some point to help him or his relations: get a charge dropped, pass a failing student, secure a passport. The principle pertains in small affairs (getting a telephone installed, obtaining a scarce train ticket during Spring Festival) to the very largest life issues involving housing, education, employment, business and politics. Naturally no society, including America's, is entirely free of this payback principle, but most highly developed nations keep it to a tolerable minimum with more stringent controls: merit systems, independent civil services, nepotism rules, regulatory agencies, and legions of lawyers and powerful court systems that offer legal redress. But China's problem is far worse—maybe not as bad as Africa's or Latin America's problem—but bad nonetheless.

Guanxi could ruin China. It's a toxin which permeates every aspect of the society. In China you don't assume that the top-level positions in business, banking, industry, education, medicine, administration, government or any other field of endeavor are held by the best, most deserving people, you assume that they are not. The best people were probably beaten out of the jobs by more skilful guanxi players. And even in instances where this is not so, instances where the most deserving person actually did get the job, the assumption is that they did not. In this respect, the guanxi system is similar to the affirmative action program in the States, it taints the deserving and the non-deserving alike. But on the whole it can be safely said that Chinese society is not being forged and led by first-rate people, but by second-raters, third-raters or worse. And that is going to have a mighty impact on China's long-term prospects.

Another pernicious effect of guanxi is that it diminishes public trust and creates armies of embittered, disaffected people. For every "winner" the guanxi system produces, there is a "loser" who missed out on the job, didn't get the scholarship, won't be moving into the spiffy new apartment. And frequently those losers were the more deserving persons—now left on the sidelines to fester and consider the injustice of it all. One wonders how long they'll take it and what implications this has for China over the long haul. Just how stable is China?

The Chinese need to ask themselves that question. They can be sure foreign investors are asking it. China's development is at a delicate stage. Foreign investment is substantial and growing, but everyone knows that stability is the sine qua non of investment, and any hint of instability scares off capital. International business and banking leaders will increasingly want assurances that China is not only stable, but also doing its utmost to coopt the best and brightest into key sectors of the economy and society. Western business and banking leaders must have full confidence in the competence of their Chinese counterparts if there is to be continued expansion of joint ventures.

I know I wouldn't have complete confidence. Of course, I can't pretend to know much about the Chinese elite in any sector of their economy or society, but I do know a little. Although I am only a small-time college professor, my doctorate and years of professional service led the Chinese Foreign Affairs Office to confer "Foreign Expert" status upon me. That status, along with the fact that the American dollar stretches a long, long way in China, has given me opportunities I would never have had elsewhere. But here and there in China I at least *see* some of the "players" in the economy and society, people who are part of the "system." Sometimes I see them in an exclusive restaurant, sometimes in a four-star hotel, sometimes in a VIP waiting lounge at an airport or train station. And I have to say, I don't always like what I see. When you see them together in a group there's something about it that reminds you of a convention of used car salesmen—albeit very successful used car salesmen. There's the same impression of shrewdness rather than intelligence. There's the same physical stuff: the embracing, the backslapping, the toothy smiles. Real cronies they are. Oh, they're breathing rarified air all right. Watching them you can almost feel what they're feeling, think what they're thinking: we're on to a good thing; we're sharing that good thing. And we'll always exclude the suckers.

The Compound

On the northeast edge of Xinxiang is the campus of Henan Normal University, home to 20,000 students, teachers and staff. Near the middle of that campus, just east of the campus auditorium and flag-raising square, is a small, walled-in patch of land. The white, concrete wall is eight-feet high and a single steel-meshed gate gives access to the area. The gate is unlocked at 6:30 each morning, and locked again at 10:30 each night. A brass plate affixed to the gate pillar reads in Chinese and English: "Foreign Affairs Office." This is where the foreigners live. This is the Foreign Compound. It used to be that each of the foreigners living here had a bodyguard to watch and guard them wherever they went. But not any more. Now we're free. At least most of the time. During the campus demonstrations and U.S. flag-burnings that followed the NATO bombing of the Chinese Embassy in Yugoslavia, the so-called "May 8th Incident," the gates were locked for three continuous days and foreigners had to stay inside their apartments and out of sight.

Come inside now, and I'll show you around. You see three white, concrete-block buildings: one in front of you and one to either side. This area in between is our garden area. There's the little grassy area just big enough for us to play badminton if we want; the flower garden where chrysanthemums are planted and bloom till the snow comes; the four tall spruce trees that anchor the clothes-lines. Actually, I'm not too crazy about this clothesline arrangement: everytime my students come to visit it seems my Fruit-of-the-Looms are hanging out there to dry. Not too dignified.

This two-story building on the left has four apartments. Its two lefthand apartments, upstairs and downstairs, are connected by an interior staircase, and are actually just one big apartment. The rooms house the offices of Mr. Li, the *waiban* (why-bon), the Chinese Foreign Affairs Officer who runs the Compound and supervises us. He's quite nice. He's in there now because that's his old bike parked by the porch. He's got a number of people to assist him. There's Yin Zhao Cun ("Richard"), a graduate student studying business management. He lives right here on the premises in the upstairs balcony apartment on the right. He's always around and is the one who locks and unlocks the gate. Li Xiao Lin is a chauffeur for university officials part of the time, and the rest of the time works as the Compound's handy-man. He mows the grass, replaces light bulbs, unclogs drains and stopped-up toilets. He's an ex-soldier and very versatile. Then there are the three women. The older one is Zhao Xinhua and she brings everyone a thermos of boiled drinking water each morning. She boils the water in the *waiban's* kitchen area. She also does general tidying up and sweeps the porches and walkways with a big old broom the business end of which is made up of three-foot-long birch twigs. The two younger women, Xue Min and Qiao Ru, serve as the *waiban's* secretaries. They type, fax, file and do the payroll. (But don't get the idea we're talking about high finance here. I'm the highest-paid person in the compound, and one of the four or five highest-paid persons in the entire university, but I'm only paid $6 a day—$3 a day once my food bill is deducted.) Actually, none of these women seem overworked. They spend a lot of their time in the *waiban's* office watching television, knitting, or, in the case of the two stylish younger women, fiddling with their hair, filing their nails, primping. They each have identical mirrors attached to the wall beside their desks. Big mirrors. Four square feet of reflective area. They look in these mirrors a lot. They'll wet a pinky and smooth down an eyebrow. They'll curl back their lips and examine their teeth. The *waiban's* office, like workplaces throughout China, is in fact overstaffed in order to give as many people as possible some employment. Everyone needs a "rice bowl." This is their "rice bowl."

The last apartment downstairs and on the right is usually vacant but is kept available for important guests and visitors. For instance last month a rich Chinese-American businessman from California stayed there several days. He was here to set up a scholarship fund for capable but extremely poor students—students having trouble feeding and clothing themselves. He also gave a couple of lectures while he was here and told the story of how he was walking around his California factory floor one day talking to his employees. He came across one young Chinese man who had gone to America on a student's visa, got himself educated, and then decided to stay on permanently. The businessman was furious, thought the young man should have been benefiting his homeland with his skills and education, and so fired him on the spot. Interesting .

Okay, now in the facing building to the right there are again four apartments. My wife and I live in the downstairs apartment on the left, and those are our two bikes on the porch. They're "Phoenixes" the Cadillacs of the Chinese bike industry. They cost me 330 yuan (U.S. $40) apiece—pretty steep. I was given the option of paying them off in monthly installments like you would a car in the States, but I paid for them with cash money in one shot. In the apartment to our right is young Adam, the other American professor, and that's his bike. Although I recommended the Phoenix to him when he first came, he decided to go with a "B.S.A." instead. Not a bad bike really, but not a Phoenix either. It confers nowhere near the same status. But I guess that's his business. To the left upstairs is Inagaki, the Japanese professor who's the same age as me, 53, while the upstairs apartment to the right is empty. It was supposed to be for a Russian piano teacher. Russians are pouring out of their bankrupt country like rats from a sinking ship, but this one only stayed in Xinxiang three days and then pulled out. He said it was too poor here and he would try his luck in eastern Europe.

Tucked away in the back there is a fourth little building you couldn't even see when you entered the Compound. It has four smaller apartments—not for foreign professors, but for rich foreign students who can afford the rent. Right now only two of the apartments are occupied: one by Yumi Okada, a Japanese girl graduate student, and the other by Chimgee Chimeddorj, a Mongol girl. I'll tell you more about them later.

Looking straight ahead you see the tiny dining hall with its three doors. The door to the left is where we eat. Wainscoted walls, chintzy drapes, one circular table with a Lazy Susan to spin the dishes. It's a dim, heatless room so cold in winter that we sit there in scarves and padded jackets. Seven of us eat there *year around,* every day, three meals a day. The same seven of us. Think about it. *Think about it.* You get to know each other awfully well, and after awhile all the easy topics are exhausted. You're left with conversations like this:

Person A: "I saw you leaving the Compound this afternoon Yumi. Where were you going?"

Yumi: "Out to the street."

Person B: "What for?"

Yumi: "To do some shopping."

Person C: "What did you buy?"

Yumi: "A pair of panties."

Person A: "What color did you get?"

Yumi: "Blue."

Person B: "What shade of blue? Light? Dark? What?"

Yumi: "Light blue."

Person C: "Why don't you go get them so we can have a look."

Next door in this middle room, the largest room, there are four circular tables where a dozen or so Nepalese undergraduate students eat. They live in a dormitory behind the Compound but come over here for their meals. These students, all boys except for Meena, Elaina and Oleeve, are part of an ongoing arrangement whereby they take a year-long crash course in Chinese before being sent to other universities and medical schools in Xi'an, Zhengzhou and elsewhere in China. Their parents send them here because this university is cheap—cheap even by Chinese standards. These Nepalese are usually very high caste Hindus and carry themselves as such. They are proud. Still, most of them get along well enough with others and the three girls have lovely dispositions. I like the way these girls dress. They are always abundantly clothed: pantaloons, skirts, saris, shawls and what not. Layers of clothes.

The girls are very polite and soft spoken. You bump into one of them swathed up outside the dining hall at night and invariably the conversation will go about like this:

"Hello Beel."

"Hello Meena."

"Is cold tonight Beel. You think is cold tonight Beel?"

"Yes, it's cold tonight Meena."

"Okay, I'm going now Beel."

"Okay, Meena."

That's how they talk.

Through the third door is the kitchen with the refrigerator, primitive stove, woks, chopping tables and so forth. Again, there is more than ample staffing. To prepare the food for the twenty people there are three male cooks: Mao Xiang, the boss cook, plus Yu Zijun and Zhang Qi. Their breakfasts are nothing special and are always the same: rice porridge, a boiled egg, bread and an apple, orange or banana. But their lunches and suppers are superb, and they have a huge repertoire of dishes used to complement rice. It is said that all three cooks were sent by the *waiban* to be trained at a four-star hotel in Zhengzhou, and I believe it. They can combine chicken, pork, fish, spinach, cabbage, potatoes, tomatoes, beans, bean sprouts, squash, mushrooms and bamboo shoots in an endless kaleidoscope of meals. The diet is nearly fat free and after three months of their cooking almost all the diners look to be at their ideal weights.

A host of food purveyors visit the kitchen each day bringing in fresh supplies. These folks are small operators and come on pedaled trishaws with their wares in the rear cargo bin. There's the milk lady who measures out milk a ladle at a time. There's the cheerful fish lady who has lined her cargo bin with a waterproof shower curtain and three or four fish swim inside. The boss cook, Mao Xiang, stands studying these with his hands in his pockets and rocks back and forth on his heels. One of the fish is a big boy, a two-footer, but he's not moving, just sort of lying there. The fish lady happily slaps him upside the head and he makes a couple of torpid swishes with his tail. Mao Xiang buys him. We've got supper.

The serving girls, Wang Ping and Wang Li, are efficient and friendly. Both are in their twenties and attractive. In fact, Wang Li is more than attractive, she's dazzling. If there were an aristocracy of looks, she'd be a queen. Very tall, slim, straight-backed and small breasted. She wears no make-up. Her clean, crisp facial features are perfect the way they are. My wife says Wang Li could have been a runway model, but this is not New York or Paris, and there are no runways around here. Instead she is our serving girl—a slender shadow, a beautiful blur that moves around the dining room at the edge of our vision. When she finishes washing the dishes she goes pedaling home on a bike too small for her long legs, with her knees bumping her chin.

The Waiban, Li Qiufa

As a foreign worker in China your relationship with your *waiban,* the Chinese Foreign Affairs Officer who is answerable to the government for you and for everything you do in China from the time you arrive until the time you leave, is the relationship that is most crucial to you. The quality of that relationship can "make" or "break" your stay in China. The *waiban* can keep you on a loose leash or a very tight one. He can be seen as an accommodating friend always there to assist you when needed, or he can be your malicious jailer. Happily, Mr. Li is the former; he is my friend, or perhaps a more accurate description of our affiliation would be to compare it to the parent-child relationship, only with the ages topsy-turvy. In this case he, the parent, is in his thirties, while I, the child, am in my fifties. If I'm lost or in trouble I carry three telephone numbers in my wallet by which I can reach him at any time, night or day. He brings me and my wife birthday cakes on our birthdays, moon cakes during Mid-Autumn Festival, cards and gifts at Christmastime. He arranges trips for us to different cities and sights, and he is always there at the Compound curbside to wave us good-bye when we leave and to greet us when we return. He brings us our mail, our pay, our holiday bonuses, our prescription drugs. One or two afternoons a week he'll stop by our apartment before supper to join us for a glass of wine and to smoke a rare cigarette. He'll use the time to cast a fatherly eye over the place: is that light bulb out? Is the radiator leaking? Are we warm enough at night? Do we need another quilt? And what does he ask in return for all this care and attention? Only that I try to do my job well and always keep him informed, as any dutiful child should, of where I'm going, what I'll be doing there, and who I'll be with . . . and to never, ever leave this city without his knowledge and permission.

Mr. Li is well educated—an English major who graduated from Henan Normal University, and who also received Russian foreign language training in turbulent Moscow following the political upheavals of 1989–1990. He is well versed not only in politics but, more to the point, in the ins and outs of government offices, banks, police stations, embassies and consulates, train stations and airports, hotels and tourist sights.

Mr. Li works very hard. For his 1000 yuan (U.S. $121) a month salary he's in his office from 8 o'clock in the morning to 6:30 or later in the evenings, and that includes most weekends too. If there are important foreign visitors he may have to show them around Beijing or Shanghai and interpret for them, in which case his working day runs far into the night. Moreover, Mr. Li not only has to look after the Compound and all its resident foreigners, its workers and dining hall staff—but he also has to manage a five-story campus hotel that has its own guest rooms, restaurant, disco bar and meeting rooms and which specializes in catering wedding parties for faculty, staff and alumni. I remember being out with Roselyn one night at a downtown Xinxiang restaurant and seeing Mr. Li there hosting a dinner with some university and city officials. The hour was late, and Mr. Li's group was an all-male affair, which necessarily meant innumerable toasts with potent Chinese wines and liquors. I had an opportunity to study Mr. Li's face at leisure. He, of course, wore his habitual good-natured smile, but anyone who knew him well could see how tired, worn and slightly befuddled he was.

You have probably realized by now that Mr. Li is a gentleman not just because he has the manners and polish to deal with VIPs, to escort and interpret for foreign guests, to introduce you to the mayor, the governor or whomever, and to do it all with admirable ease, but also because he is a gentleman in spirit. He never willingly gives offense to anyone. He is tolerant, even-tempered, sympathetic. He never stands on his dignity. If that fluorescent light is out and Xiao Li and Richard aren't around, he'll show up with tube in hand and put it in himself. Or, after dinner at the Compound, seeing Meena, Oleeve and Elaina cheerfully skipping rope, he'll come over and join in. He laughs; he's happy. But if you want to see him at his happiest, you'd have to see him with his wife. He glows in her presence. He dotes on her. She is a tiny little elf of a creature who teaches singing and dancing at a nearby primary school. In the Li's tiny apartment, kept neat as a pin, sits a gleaming white piano—a piano workmen wrestled up six flights of stairs with Mr. Li bobbing about making sure it received not a single scratch. After dinner with the Li's she will play for you and sing for you in her lovely, unbelievably high, soprano voice. Mr. Li will laugh. He will be happy.

Roselyn Adams

My wife is no baby, but she cried our first night in the Compound. She sat in a chair and wept. I asked her why she was crying; she said she didn't know. I think I know. Part of it was the hassle-ridden day that culminated in the flight from Shanghai and the two-hour car trip from Zhengzhou Airport to Xinxiang—a road trip that first brought home to us the shattering poverty of interior China where so many lives are led on the bare edge of subsistence, and part of it was the release of tension that came after living out of suitcases in an exhausting month of "vacationing" enroute to China with stops at Taipei, Singapore, Kuala Lumpur and Tioman Island off the coast of Malaysia. And part of it was seeing the Compound apartment for the first time. It's not such a bad place really—we've got a little living room, a little bedroom, a little study, a little bathroom. But everything *is* little, and living in a 500-square-foot apartment after being used to your own home three or four times that large does take some getting used to as does having no hot water (except from 6:00 to 9:00 in the evening) and no kitchen. With no job per se at the university, Roselyn would be on an enforced "holiday" for the first time in her life, and she had so looked forward to "her kitchen," and to shopping at the market and cooking Chinese for me. And now she found she wouldn't even have that outlet. And then, too, there was the matter of the apartment's decor. Roselyn is artistic and has always prided herself on creating lovely homes for us wherever we've lived. She prides herself on her living rooms especially—where we will spend most of our hours, where we will receive our guests. Always she has created warm, atmospheric living rooms with her candles, her photographs, her knickknacks, her little "appointments." But what she faced here buckled her knees: a living room with three tan walls and one of lime green, putrid pea-green doors and door jambs, sky-blue venetian blinds and ceiling moldings, bright red carpeting, and an ultra-modern, aerodynamic-looking living room suite upholstered in bold tan and turquoise checks. The overall impression was that a peacock must have somehow wandered into the room and exploded. And the living room was just for starters, and "appetizer" so to speak. As further investigation was to prove, in the more private rooms—the study, the bedroom, the bathroom—rooms only the tenants were intended to fully appreciate and enjoy, the deranged decorator decided to really cut himself loose and the counterpoising of electric blue with peppermint pink formed his principal motif. Roselyn's pronouncement: "Crackhouse chic."

But, of course, the most important cause of Roselyn's first night weeping was the realization that this was to be "home" for a year, and she was 10,000 miles away from her real home and our two children. Roselyn, however, is nothing if not resilient, and after a good night's sleep she steadied up and cheerfully started cleaning and organizing, prepared to make the best of what she had.

How does one describe a wife—a loyal wife of thirty-some years, a wife with whom a man has shared all the vicissitudes of his life? It is sad, but true, that such a wife becomes so completely a part of you, so essentially a part of you, that she can sometimes be taken for granted. She is like your right arm—or your heartbeat. And how often do you really take notice of your right arm? How often do you listen to your heartbeat? One has occasionally to take a step or two back to see in full the wife he has.

I met Roselyn in 1968 when I was a young naval officer and my carrier, the U.S.S. *Forrestal,* anchored off Marseilles, France, after some months at sea. I hadn't seen or spoken to a female in so long that on my first afternoon of shore liberty I went to a Marseilles nightclub to see if I could meet a girl. There were girls there naturally, but they were all French. I couldn't speak to any of them. However, I noticed that the disc jockey was English, and I asked him if he knew of any English-speaking girls that I might meet. He told me that two Scottish girls usually came to the club at a certain hour of the evening, and so I returned to the club a little before that time and took a table where I could watch the door. I knew immediately that it was them when they came in—they had that British "look." And I also knew which of the two I liked: the smaller, fairer one with the close-cropped tawny hair who had a jaunty attitude about her and who smiled easily. I asked her to dance. I learned she was an au pair girl who had just quit her job and would be leaving Marseilles in two nights time with her girlfriend. Two nights later I got shore liberty again and saw her off on the first stage of their journey—they had bought space in the cab of a coal truck departing for Paris that night. I waved them good-bye. Roselyn and I promised to write. Three days later my ship returned to sea.

And one would naturally have thought our friendship would have ended there. But it did not. We did write. In the months that followed once a week there would be a letter for me when the mail plane touched down on the flight deck. I remember those letters well. The pale blue envelopes marked "Air Mail; Par Avion"; the stamps bearing Queen Elizabeth's serene profile; my name and address written in the neat, straight up-and-down, almost childlike script. I still keep those letters bundled up in a box and reread them once or twice a decade. It was through those letters that I came to know Roselyn. Each letter was like a piece of a picture puzzle, and once I had enough of those pieces I could make out the picture sufficiently well to know this was a person I could love. Of course I knew I'd never own all the pieces of this puzzle, nor did I wish to. But I had enough. When my year-long cruise ended and the carrier returned to its homeport in Norfolk, Virginia, I flew to Glasgow and we were married. I doubt we had been as much as 24 hours in each other's physical presence when we took our vows.

We have had a good life together—and we have kept our vows. We have raised two decent children to adulthood and independence. We have travelled a good deal: six continents, 40 countries, 48 of the American states. Roselyn's wanderlust eventually wore itself out, but mine never has and probably never will.

In our married life we've lived in Virginia, North Dakota, New York, Oklahoma and Texas and have worked 13 years abroad in Portugal, Australia (three different stays), the Solomon Islands and China. During those years Roselyn has encouraged me to pursue my dreams wherever they might take me and faithfully followed in my meandering footsteps filling whatever role fate has handed her: a Navy wife, a college student, a teacher's wife, professor's wife, a mother, a housekeeper, and, usually too, a secondary breadwinner. She has worked at various times as a restaurant waitress (in North Dakota) where she had to wear a corny, calico farm girl's costume which she hated; an insurance company clerk (New York); art teacher (Australia); a housekeeper for Catholic monks (Australia); English teacher at a jungle mission school (Solomon Islands); and art gallery manager (Texas). And, during one bleak, six-month period of our lives back in 1984 when a couple of back-to-back runs of bad luck found me supporting our family on a $400-a-month paycheck earned shifting sacks of manure and assembling lawn-mowers in the garden section of a Guthrie, Oklahoma, Wal-Mart store, she'd join me two nights a week laid out on hideous transfu-sion recliners in a miserable Oklahoma City plasma center where we'd sell our blood plasma for $10 a crack. I tried to persuade her to let me do that alone, but she insisted she go along too. Oh, those were horrible nights. Three hours you'd lie there alongside the scores of other poor blood sellers who frankly looked to be and, in most cases, were human refuse. A vein would be tapped, a quart of blood slowly drained off into a bag, the bag taken to a lab where the plasma was centrifuged out, your then depleted blood slowly dripped back into your arm, the one-hour recovery period so you wouldn't faint when you stood up. And all the while the inescapable TV sets affixed to the ceiling would be blaring—invariably tuned to "The Jetsons" or some other inane program tailored for a moron audience. Then the long, light-headed drive home with bandaged arms. It was awful. It was demeaning. But Roselyn never once complained, never once gave me an accusing glance, never once suggested that I was a lousy provider for her and the kids. She knew just how fragile my ego had become in those days, and never let on that she was anything less than proud of her husband.

During the course of our life together I think what I have found most endearing in my wife is her love of people. There's her mother's love for her children of course, and this is absolute and unconditional. Had either or both of our children turned out to have been ax-murderers I don't think it would have fazed Roselyn one whit. Her nimble mind would have quickly found some sort of an excuse for them—likely the victims would have "deserved what they got." But beyond this love is her love for the helpless, for the underdogs, in all forms and fashions: old people, children, the poor, the retarded . . . a lonesome parrot in a cage that's plucked out its own tail feathers in despair. In extending her love, Roselyn is the very antithesis of a snob. In her role as art gallery manager in Brownsville she numbered the window cleaner and the UPS deliveryman amongst her closest friends. She kept photos of them and their families, would remember them on their birthdays and so forth. She had a soft spot too for the legions of door-to-door salespeople who try to scratch a living in Brownsville—poor people who stand on your doorstep trying to interest you in their homemade tamales, enchiladas, cookies, fish cakes or what have you. Our refrigerator was always crammed full of these unwanted, never-to-be-eaten foods.

Closely related to Roselyn's love of people is her amazing facility for remembering people's names, faces, and personal trivia. She'll know, for instance, that this customer is divorced, has two children, the oldest of which is studying to be a cosmetologist. "Who cares?" would be my response. Who wants to clog up their mind with such minutiae? Well, my wife, for one, does.

In the Compound here in Xinxiang, Roselyn has quickly found her niche. She may have no formal job, but she's busy nonetheless—helping me, helping others. She has made a lovely home out of the unpromising apartment. It's tidy. And atmospheric. There are photographs of our children and friends all over the place. We have potted plants, flowers and knickknacks galore: souvenir plates, Chinese fans, calligraphy scrolls, incense burners, you name it. Roselyn is also big on candles and two or three burn every evening in the living room. The students who nightly come to visit us to practice their spoken English are fascinated by these candles. At first they were a bit concerned that the candles *were* being burned at all since in a Chinese home candles are only lit if the electricity is out or to connote that a dead body is present in the house. But the students have caught on quickly, and Roselyn's evening candles delight them: "How romantic!" they say. Roselyn also keeps a good stock of candies, cookies and fruits on hand for our student visitors. She is always very welcoming to them, and they love her in return. Often there will be a dozen or more students in the house of an evening, and it is Roselyn who they most want to see. I'm of a somewhat taciturn nature, so it is Roselyn's chair that they most often bunch up around. And it's not boring academic topics that she raises with them, but things that interest the kids far more: "Who knit you that pretty sweater?"; "Are you getting homesick?"; "Did you get any letters this week?"

I have seven classes of students—310 students in all—and in my study I have a photograph of each student holding beneath their chin a cardboard strip with their chosen English name printed upon it. Now it is my duty, my business, to know my students' names and faces and I have devoted a good deal of effort in doing so, but what pleases me is that Roselyn has also made it her business. She has studied the photos and used her facility for remembering names and faces to learn all of them. It is so gratifying to these typically shy students, usually of peasant stock, to be greeted by name at the door and warmly invited in.

Another duty Roselyn has voluntarily undertaken is assisting me in my grading. With 310 students—160 of whom are taking my English Writing course—the grading threatened to overwhelm me. So Roselyn has taken over much of that chore, particularly the grading of diaries. With 160 students required to maintain diaries, and each to make a nightly entry of not less than 100 words, 16,000 words are generated each day that have to be checked. Roselyn does much of this, carefully making the tedious red-ink corrections to grammar and spelling, and also penning expressions of sympathy or encouragement to the homesick, the lovesick, the girl depressed about being ugly, the boy fearing he is failing. So many young people; so many worries. And the diarists are so grateful that they are being "listened to" that many have come to use their diaries as a source of advice—a personal "Dear Abby" line: "Roselyn, what should I do about this?"; "Roselyn, what can I do about that?" All receive a reply. And in cases of actual need—needs invariably conveyed in the diaries of a classmate or dormmate and never in the diary of the needy student him—or herself—the destitute girl who is eating scraps picked out of canteen garbage cans, the boy who hasn't a coat, the fatherless girl who lacks train fare to visit her bedridden mother—Roselyn will inform me so that an envelope can be discreetly tucked into that student's diary when it is returned.

And that's Roselyn: a wife for all seasons.

Hu Rui-Juan—"Helen"

Shuffle, shuffle. Listen. Scuffle, scuffle. Listen! Famous feet are wiping themselves. Happiness is in the air. The door opens and a beaming face appears from behind it. "It's me." Yes, it's her. It's our Helen. Our dear daughter is home for the day.

The best part of the day now begins. She goes into the study and hangs her coat on her coathook. She drops her scarf, mittens, bookbag and water flask beside the desk. She comes back into the living room and throws herself down on the couch. She plucks an orange from the fruit basket and begins to peel it. We talk about her day. "What did you eat for lunch, Helen?" "I ate noodle." "Who'd you eat with?" "I ate noodle with Jennifer in Number Three Canteen." "Where did you study today, Helen?" "I studied in the library until lunch and in Number One Building in the afternoon. I studied all day." She bounds off the couch to plug a cassette into the recorder. She sings along; she whistles; she prances and dances around a bit. She's lovely. I sit sipping a beer while Roselyn sits knitting. Helen entertains us until suppertime. While we are in the dining hall she unbraids her long, long pigtail and washes her hair, takes her shower. When we return she is reseated with her flowing hair fanned out across her back to dry, and she uses her chopsticks to quickly scoop up the bowlful of food we've pilfered for her from the dining room. At 7 o'clock she resumes work in the backroom study while Roselyn and I begin to greet the sophomore students who have come to practice their English. Sometimes Helen comes out to join the conversation for awhile, sometimes not, although al-

most always she'll make some sort of appearance if to do nothing more than to let people see she is a member of our family and to demonstrate her proprietary rights. If students stay beyond 10 o'-clock, she may come out to remind them that it's time for them to leave: "Okay, it's time for Bill and Roselyn to rest." She, herself, stays until ten minutes before the 11 o'clock dormitory curfew for seniors. She then bundles up in her coat and mittens, and wraps the scarf Roselyn knitted for her around her neck and face right up to her eyes. We each embrace her—hold her for a long moment—then let her go. She boards her bike while I unlock the Compound gate, then she's gone . . . until tomorrow. Always tomorrow.

We first decided to bring Helen home to the states with us following a five-day trip to Xi'an in which, with the *waiban's* approval, Helen accompanied Roselyn, Adam and me as our guide and interpreter. You get to know someone very well under such intimate circumstances—sharing meals, train compartments and hotel rooms—and are together every waking and sleeping moment. And Helen did her job so well, so conscientiously. She carried a notebook with pages filled in her crimped handwriting of information she had researched in advance: "The Big Wild Goose Pagoda was constructed in such and such dynasty. According to legend such and such happened there." When souvenir hunting we'd enter a shop separately, like we weren't together. When the shopkeeper's head was turned we'd point to what we wanted and leave. Helen would emerge with the item and a triumphant smile a few minutes later, having paid a third of what an American tourist would have paid. She even worked out a restroom system for her and Roselyn to use. Helen would go in first and scope things out. Roselyn would watch from across the crowded restaurant. If Helen emerged with her arms at her sides that was the green light for Roselyn to come ahead; crossed arms meant a no-no. The whole trip was delightful and made much more so by Helen's unfailing cheeriness—her singing, her whistling, her affectionate clinging to arms wherever we might go.

In our decision to make Helen a part of the family, one crystalizing moment came for me on the night train home from Xi'an. In our sleeping compartment Helen was in the top right bunk, Roselyn in the bottom right. I was in the bottom left bunk with Adam above me. From my position I could keep watch on both Roselyn and Helen during the seemingly endless night of fitful sleep—stops and starts, rough sections of track, mournful train whistles. At one point during the wee hours Helen climbed down the ladder to use the toilet. When she came back she noticed Roselyn's blanket had slipped off. She recovered Roselyn and tucked her in with such tenderness before crawling back up to her own bunk. She laid there on her stomach with her face pressed to the window watching her country slide by in the night. She watched and watched, watching something new, watching her world. And all the while I was watching her—watching the moonlight reflecting off that flat oriental face, watching those glycerin, almond eyes. I knew then I wanted her to be with us for as long as we could have her.

Unfortunately, getting Helen into the States just for a two-year stay while she undertakes an English master's program is no easy matter because there is something seriously wrong with America's visa granting criteria. U.S. consular officers seem to thirst for Caribbeans (frequently criminals) and Latinos (often illiterates) while abhorring Asians with sterling credentials. Still, we are optimistic that Helen's ability and promise are so evident that the U.S. Visa Unit at Beijing will, however reluctantly, feel compelled to grant her a student's visa. Consider for a moment a sampling of her achievements which I mentioned in my letter of recommendation for her to graduate school (keeping in mind that I discarded more than a dozen awards she had won in gymnastics, track, and singing): ranked first academically in the Foreign Language Department of Henan Normal University (HNU) every year 1996 to 1999; "First Prize, English Speech Contest" (HNU), 1998; "The Excellent Leader Prize" of the Student Union (HNU), 1998; "First Prize Rifle Marksmanship," HNU Military Reserve Brigade of the People's Liberation Army, 1997; "First Prize, Xinxiang City Dancing Competition," 1997; "Second Prize, Henan Province Dancing Competion," 1997 (Remember there are 103 million people in the province); "The Excellent Member Prize" of the Communist Youth League (HNU) in both 1997 and 1998; "The Excellent Provincial College Girl Student Prize," Henan Province, 1998. Who could refuse her?

I don't know whether Helen is beautiful or not—certainly she is beautiful in *our* eyes—but we are too close to her to be objective. She herself does not think she is. Sometimes she derides her "moon face," and once when I suggested to her she might want to consider using her language abilities (she also speaks Russian) to become an air hostess, she dismissed the notion out of hand muttering something about China Airlines only wanting "pretty" girls. And I suppose, too, Helen's figure might not come up to the slender, willowy ideal of, say, a model. Helen is only of medium height, and she's not that slender—in particular, her buttocks and thighs are very sturdy and heavily muscled as befits a dancer and a gymnast.

But I would defy anyone not to find Helen beautiful once they knew her. She has a personality that absolutely glows, and she radiates happiness wherever she goes, whatever she does. She's so *vital*. She's smiling, chuckling, whistling, singing virtually the whole day long. Chirpy as a bird. Fooling around with her mouth a while back she developed a little trick whereby she puts her tongue on the roof of her mouth, creates some kind of a suction vacuum in there, and then suddenly releases the tongue with great force. It produces a loud, *really* loud, "tok" noise. "TOK! You can hear it a block away. So she uses it to startle friends, babies, donkeys, animals at the zoo. She'll nuzzle up to your ear and "TOK!" It shatters your nerves and jollies her up no end. I tell her to "Stop making that stupid noise!" And what do I get? "TOK! TOK! TOK! TOK! TOK!" Five toks. She's hopeless. I once asked her if she's *always* happy? She smiled and fluttered her eyelids, Helen language for "yes." "Are you ever *unhappy?*" "Sometimes when I'm having my natural period I cry. I don't know why."

And she's always so unaffected. There's never a false note with her. She's reading a book in the living room and comes across the term "freshen up." She asks me what this means. I tell her it's a euphemism for using the toilet. "Okay, I'm going to 'freshen up.'" She bounds out of her seat, goes to the bathroom. "Bang!" That's the lid going up, then the sound of her making water. She's completely nonchalant about all bodily functions.

Helen is also a very physical person, and I'm not referring here so much to her dancing, gymnastics and athletics, although that is probably one expression of it, but to her need, like so many Chinese, for physical contact with other people. If she's walking with someone—her girlfriends, her classmates, Roselyn, me her Chinese parents, whomever, she'll almost always have a hold of their arm. She likes to touch people. She's always pulling people up out of their chairs, tagging behind them and pushing them in this direction or that, bundling babies and children about, tickling them. If she's sitting next to a girlfriend, her hand will be somewhere on that girl—her knee, her shoulder, her hair. And Helen likes to be touched too. Sometimes she'll sit at the foot of my living room chair and rest her head against my knee. I'll stroke her hair like a cat. She doesn't purr . . . but almost. She hums, drifts into a sort of reverie. Helen is a virgin and has never had any romantic contacts with boys to speak of. Her Chinese parents would never allow her to see boys when she was at home, and here at the university, where she is a campus leader and probably the most prominent single student—the student the administrative leaders hold up as a role model for each incoming freshman class—she has had to conform to their dictates of leaving romance aside and concentrating on study. But I worry how all this is going to play out in her future, in light of her physical needs, her need to touch and be touched. She worries herself. I remember one conversation Roselyn and I had with her on the topic. Helen's standing, talking, hands in motion as always when she's talking. She's telling us of her plan to put off marriage until she's 30 so she can concentrate on building a career. She's very emotional; her eyes have watered and are glistening. "How am I going to make it until I'm 30 without . . . (Here she pauses while searching for the right word.) . . . without enjoying myself with a boy? How am I going to be able to do that?" Her arms are stretched straight out, palms open, crucifixion style.

You know, Helen can also be fiery at times. And when her "blood's up" the high ridges of her cheekbones just below the eyes turn ruby red. I remember one evening during oral English practice with the students in the living room there was one student present who I really don't like—a sly, uncouth, misfit of a student—and neither does Helen. Without asking, he picked up a framed photo of Helen we have sitting on the coffee table. Helen saw this and her ridges went ruby in a flash. She snatched the picture out of his hand and shoved him in his shoulder. "Don't you touch my picture! Don't you look at my picture! I don't want you ever to look at me!"

Another night when she was walking rather than biking back to her dorm, a boy cycled past her, shot out his hand and touched her on the breast. She screamed at him, looked for something to throw, and, lo and behold, found a fist-sized chuck of brick immediately to hand. She walloped him square in the back. Yelping in triumph, she then tore off after him calling him every bad name she could think of. He pedaled away in panic. Now how many girls do you know with that kind of spirit?

I once found myself on the receiving end of Helen's fieriness. I was sitting across the coffee table from her picking through some photos a photographer had donated to me that morning. These were photos taken two months before our arrival in China and were of the demonstrations and American flag burnings which occurred on our campus following the May 8th Incident. I was concentrating my attention on one particular photograph: a massive march of the university's students down a Xinxiang boulevard. The photographer had gained an elevated point to take the picture and shot down and in to the sea of students. They were marching twenty abreast, and the column stretched down the boulevard as far as the eye could see. Some were carrying banners—written in Chinese characters. I pointed to one banner and asked Helen what it said.

"It says: Death to NATO." (Her cheek ridges begin to rouge up.)

"My God. Don't they realize the bombing was a mistake? Everyone in the West knew it was a mistake immediately. Who put the students up to this? Who organized this march? Who is at the head of the column leading it?"

No answer. Silence. And then something clicked in my head ... The Excellent Member Prize of the Communist Youth League ... The Excellent Leader Prize of the Student Union. I looked up into Helen's eyes and then I knew. "Helen, it's you that organized this march. It's you that's at the head of the column leading it. Isn't it?"

(Helen's cheek ridges are red now.) "You Americans were killing us Chinese. We had to do something. I was a leader of the Student Union."

"Yes Helen. But don't you know it was a mistake? It was a terrible mistake. They hit the wrong building."

"It was *no* mistake! American's too developed. It has too much technology. It couldn't make a mistake like that." (Ridges aflame.)

"But why, Helen? Why would America do that? It makes no sense. America doesn't want China as an enemy."

"To teach us a lesson."

"What lesson? What lesson, Helen?"

"To teach us to keep down! To teach us not to rise up! You Americans, you Europeans, you NATO want to keep China down. You'll never allow us to be your equals."

"Oh Helen, that's not true. That's not true."

"It is true. It is. But let's not talk about it anymore." (The flames begin to wane.)

It's a lazy Sunday afternoon the day after Christmas. Kirstin, our number one daughter, has flown over from the States for the holiday season. Helen, our number two daughter, has put a "do not disturb" sign up on our door in Chinese. We lounge about the living room. Kirstin and I are cross-legged on the carpet putting a puzzle together. Roselyn is in one easy chair knitting, while number two daughter is sprawled in the other reading J.D. Salinger's *Catcher in the Rye,* a gift Kirstin brought for her from the States. Helen's knowledge of formal English is excellent, but she has limited understanding of the American vernacular. Everytime she comes across a new word she looks up to ask its meaning. "'He was a flitty looking guy.' What does that mean?" We tell her. "Okay, we have those in China too." She reads a while. "What does 'dope' mean?" We tell her. "Okay, thanks dopes." That's one of the really irritating things about Helen: whenever she learns a new word, she uses it over and over again for the next few days in order to cement it into her vocabulary. She reads on. "'Puke.' 'It makes you want to puke.' What does that mean?" Someone says to take the book away from her, but she resists, "No, no. I like it." Next it's "wolf." "What does it mean to 'wolf down' food?" It's explained. She begins to peel an orange. "Okay you dopes, I'm going to wolf down this orange." She eats and goes right on talking, showing us her mouthful of orange pulp. "Does it make you dopes want to puke watching me wolf down this orange?" A little bit later: "It says here this boy 'ripped one off and damn near blew the roof off.' What does that mean?" Roselyn drops her knitting in her lap in despair. Kirstin rolls her eyes back into her head. Time passes. Then Helen announces, "Okay dopes, I'm going to freshen up." She heads for the toilet. Just before she closes the door she pokes her head back out: "Don't worry dopes, I'm not going to blow the roof off." You can hear her in there chuckling, enormously pleased with herself. What are we going to do with her?

That's our Helen. Sunshine on our souls.

Adam Branson

Even before we arrived in Xinxiang Roselyn and I were apprised by the *waiban* that one other American would be joining the University's tiny foreign community. This would be Adam. Naturally Roselyn and I hoped he would be both a man we liked and a man we'd be proud to claim as a fellow American. Our hopes were wonderfully fulfilled and, if memory serves, those are exactly the sentiments we penned on his "Birthday Banner" when the Compound celebrated his 24th.

Seldom, in my many years of teaching experience, have I seen a first-year teacher "take" to teaching as successfully as young Adam. I've seen some awfully hard-working teachers fail in their first year because they lacked people skills, and likewise I've seen teachers with exceptional personal rapport with their students, at least initially, fail over the long haul of the academic year because they neglected the tedious chores of planning good lessons and tests and were lazy about grading and correcting students' work. Adam, however, not only has  superb people skills, but is a very hard worker as well. The students, of course, love him.

To tell the truth, I'm a little jealous. Put yourself in my shoes. Aside from other duties, Adam and I both teach the 160 sophomore English majors. He takes them for Oral English, I for Written English. (We both work with them on informal oral English at night.) So when I collect their diaries I've got 160 students, mainly females, contrasting the two of us. Here's him: "young and handsome"; "lovely smile"; "beautiful blonde hair"; "long golden eyelashes"; "all the girls love him"; "we all loved him immediately"; "handsome boy-angel"; "some of my dormmates put on their most fashionable clothes whenever they have Adam's class." I have to read this crud.

Here's me: "old and gray"; "very old"; "strict looking"; "very strict looking"; "drastic looking"—*drastic* for God's sake; "has a long nose like we know foreigners are supposed to have"; "a little frightening"; "Sir, could you please smile more"; "a kindly old gentleman." That last little ninny learned just how kindly I could be when she got back her diary grade.

One thing that really got to me was the way a casual agreement Adam and I made panned out. For our first few months on the job we decided we'd stand together at the English class building entrance and greet our students as they entered each morning. We thought this

would be a good way to learn the students' names while simultaneously buoying up their day and showing them what jolly good fel-
lows we were. I must be stupid. Any dolt could have foreseen the
consequences: oodles of students ganged up around the boy-angel to
enjoy his golden eyelashes and lovely smile while I might have been
a lamppost anchored there for all anyone cared. After a few weeks
Adam, no doubt out of pity for me, aborted the practice.

Now I know I'm beginning to sound petty, but another thing
that irked me was the Thanksgiving Concert. I still feel angry and
wronged when I think about it. The Foreign Language Department
hosted this campus-wide evening event in the University auditorium at which a dozen or so songs, dances and skits would be
performed before several hundred mainly non-English-speaking
students and faculty members. I was invited to prepare an appro-
priate opening address, and I did so. I worked hard on it, and I delivered it with Helen standing at my side to render it into Chinese
with every pause and nuance intact. It was standard boilerplate actually, but it hit all the right buttons: "so much for both nations to
be thankful for" . . . "peace" . . . "prosperity" . . . "growing ties of
friendship." I thought my ending quite rousing: "God Bless
America!" [Then a critical pause here to inject just the right amount
of suspense into the easily anticipated close . . . wait for it . . . wait
for it.] "GOD BLESS CHINA!!" How could I miss? I couldn't.
The applause was gratifying, very gratifying.

Helen and I resumed our front row seats beside Roselyn. I
sank into my chair feeling quite satisfied. I sat with my elbows on
the armrests and my palms together prayer-style tapping my pursed
lips with my fingertips. I expected to feel more deeply satisfied any
moment . . . and that was because Adam was to give the first performance, and I knew it was going to be a shambles.

The students had succeed in persuading Adam to sing a solo in
Chinese . . . in *Chinese* mind you. He had deep misgivings about
this since he realized his Chinese was poor, his singing ability nil,
and his stage persona before such a large audience a complete un-
known. In the days leading up to the concert he conveyed his misgivings to me, spoke of canceling out, but I, seeing that this had
"disaster" written all over it, encouraged him to go ahead: "You'll be
all right once you're out there on the stage . . . The kids are really
going to appreciate your making the effort."

So there I sat, and now Adam came out. Things started well. He came forward in a strange sort of sideways crouch with panicky-eyes and his mouth gaping like a corpse's rictus . . . with no sound coming out. He had forgotten to turn on his microphone. By the time the emcee could skip across the stage and fix this, boy-angel was in deep trouble, thrashing about totally out of sync with the music. Joy, pure and sweet, blossomed in my soul. But what really *thrilled* me was his voice when it *could* be heard: it was *awful;* stark staring awful; a tuneless, twangy, gibberish—not Chinese, not anything. And watching him creep about the stage in that sideways crab crawl was truly rich. How would he ever survive the shame and ridicule this performance would bring him? Would he slit his wrists tonight? Would I be over in his apartment tomorrow with a bucket and mop cleaning up the mess?

And then it happened. I don't know why or how really, but the boy-angel was starting to win them over. Maybe they felt sorry for him, maybe they admired his stubborn courage for going ahead with such a desperate performance, maybe it was that hokey, farm-boy smile of his. Who knows? But for whatever reason, people were beginning to get behind him: clapping with the music, shouting out encouragement. A movement started. (I looked around wondering what was wrong with these people, and vaguely wondering if there were any way I could stop them. But, no, this was an irresistible force too big for anyone to stop.) And Adam began to feed off the crowd's support. He began to sing and move about the stage with real enthusiasm. The singing was just as terrible as ever, the movements were just as spastic as ever, but enthusiasm was there. Together the two, Adam and the audience, in horrible harmony, worked towards the song's hideous crescendo. Then silence. One second passed, two seconds passed, three seconds passed. And then it came: a tidal wave of applause. THUNDEROUS! Absolutely THUNDEROUS! The emcee rushed forward to shake Adam's hand and spoke of how everyone—especially the girls— were enraptured by his performance. Adam took bow after bow wearing that big dorky smile. My speech was forgotten in a minute—in an instant. It was like it was nothing—had never been. Can you blame me for being bitter? This was so unjust. Do I sound mean spirited?

Chimeddorj Chimgee

One hot August day in 1999 the *waiban* entered the dining room at suppertime. At his side was a sloe-eyed girl dressed in a frilly summer smock. Her skin was the fairest I've ever seen, literally snow-white. She was Chimgee, freshly arrived from the Mongolian capital of Ulan Bator.  Since she knew no Chinese and had only a smattering of English, communication was an immediate problem. Her Mongolian was useless in this situation, as was her fluent Russian once the trilingual *waiban* had introduced her and departed. A place was set for her at our circular table, and there she was seated. She began to eat in silence, keeping her head down. She was nervous, as was evidenced by the trembling tips of her chopsticks.

But in our tiny group no one could possibly feel nervous for long and the ice was quickly broken. With our mishmash of languages and our well-practiced pantomime skills we soon squeezed out Chimgee's "story." She was 23 years old and of the Mongolian middle class—her father being a mechanical engineer and her mother a businesswoman. Chimgee had spent her childhood in Moscow and had absorbed the language as only a child can, but back home in Ulan Bator her Russian language expertise was now of declining value. With the political and economic collapse of Russia, Mongolia no longer had to tailor its politics and economy to suit the stumbling giant to its north, but to suit the rising giant to its south: China. Chimgee had come to learn Chinese.

By the second day of her stay we had progressed to more personal questions. We asked about her amazing alabaster skin and the very slight curl to her hair—so rare amongst Mongoloid peoples. We point to her hair: "Is the wave in your hair real? Is it natural?" "Yes. Ees real. Ees natural. Mudder Russian." By the same token she was becoming quite comfortable with us. She, whose limbs are perfectly hairless, wanted to examine us hairy Caucasians. She brushed the hairs on my arms with the tips of her fingers then suddenly grabbed a handful and pulled till the hair follicles stood up in peaks. She giggled, sniggered actually, with a sort of horrible fascination, covering her mouth with her hand as she did so. [It's curious that: that spontaneous, subconscious gesture we humans make to conceal our mouths, our grins, whenever we are delighted by someone else's misfortunes.] Next Chimgee pulled up Adam's trouser leg to disclose a hairy calf. She grabbed a fistful of hair and tugged on it. This was too much for poor Chimgee. She exploded in laughter. She was living with freaks.

Within two weeks Chimgee was completely absorbed into our Compound group, and thumping us all at ping-pong. When we asked her if she knew how to play, she indicated a space of an inch with her thumb and forefinger and said, "a leetle." By the end of the day she was our new champion—slamming everything that came at her.

We're seated at our outdoor beer place on the street where Chimgee can hold her own with the best of us. "Hey Chimgee, why aren't you smiling? Down in the dumps? Homesick for the steppes? For your yurt? Dreaming of drinking yak blood? Isn't that what you people live on?"

Chimgee's caught just two words of this: "Yurt yees! Yak yees! We like!" She chortles.

Genghis Khan.

Okada Yumi

Yumi, the 24-year-old Japanese graduate student, is from Hiroshima. And, believe me, no word produces more of a jolt in an American-Japanese conversation than that city's name. Five minutes into our first conversation: "Where in Japan are you from Yumi?" "Hiroshima." Bang! You veer towards a safer topic—any topic? And you never return to that topic. At least that is the way it has been.

Yumi is the product of a middle-class family; her parents own and operate a construction supply business. She received a bachelor's degree in law from a Japanese university in 1998, then came to China to study the Chinese language. First she studied in Xi'an, Shanxi Province, then, after a year, came to Xinxiang in July, 1999.

Xi'an University had many Japanese students in residence, whereas in Xinxiang she would be in a class of one and able to get individual tutoring. She's a good student. You can see her intelligence in everything she does. Around the Compound dining table, she's one of the most "useful" diners, since, aside from Krishna, she's the only one proficient in all three languages used at the table: English, Chinese and Japanese. Eventually she will return to Japan to work as a tour guide catering to Chinese and English speaking visitors.

Yumi is well known to the Chinese students on campus, particulary the girl students, because although most of the Chinese have a deep antipathy towards the Japanese—their World War II oppressors—they do respect and admire Japan's wealth and modernity. In matters of fashion, they see the Japanese as the oriental pacesetters. So the Chinese girls are always fascinated by what Yumi's wearing, how she's doing her hair, what eye shadow, lipstick and nail polish she has on. (Most of the Chinese girls wear little or no make-up. In fact one of my senior girls was subjected to official "criticism" for being too heavily made-up.) They are also titillated when they see Yumi sitting with us other foreigners at our outdoor beer place just off campus—drinking and smoking in public. How dashing! And, most of all, the Chinese girls admire and envy Yumi for attracting and winning the heart of the delectable Adam.

Interestingly, Yumi has an older brother who pitches for the Toyota Corporation's baseball team. I say "interestingly" because Yumi inherited no athletic prowess whatsoever. None.

You ought to see her play ping-pong. She begins by holding the paddle up in front of her face like a hand mirror—the way a six year old would. Next, she pokes her tongue out of the corner of her mouth and clamps it there in concentration. Then, finally, she lobs the ball up to you so soft and slow it looks like a fat, juicy peach hanging there. You can do whatever you want with it: slam it to the left, slam it to the right, slam it off her forehead if you like. Some of the Compound "softies" like Adam and Inagaki let her win some points, try to keep it close, boost her along by saying things like, "Nice try Yumi," "Way to go Yumi," "Keep it up Yumi," and other such rubbish, but I don't think coddling is good for her. So what, if she's little? So what, if she's inexperienced? She's and adult and needs to learn that life can be hard. And I enjoy teaching her. I'll beat her 21-zip if I can, or, more usually, something like 21-3. I'm willing to trade off three or four points if I can get in a few good headshots along the way.

Fortunately, Yumi has a good sense of humor. She laughs easily and often, and her laugh, like her voice, is surprisingly deep and rich—a là Lauren Bacall. However Yumi, un-Bacall-like, blushes very easily. "Hey, Yumi, it's Saturday. Watcha doing tonight? Gonna chug saki till you're stupid . . . again?" Nice laugh. [Wait just a moment. It's coming.] Very nice blush.

Inagaki Itsuo

In the apartment immediately above Roselyn and me lives the youthful, 53-year-old professor of Japanese, Inagaki. He comes from Suzuka City in Japan's Mie Prefecture, a prefecture which has an ongoing teacher exchange program with China's Henan Province. Inagaki is the president of that exchange program, and is one of the teachers currently on exchange, serving his second year at Henan Normal University. He has about thirty Chinese students at various levels whom he is currently instructing in Japanese. He is a popular teacher with over three decades of teaching experience to draw upon, and students in ones, twos and threes are constantly trekking up the metal staircase outside our window for individual or group tutorial sessions in his apartment. The staircase rings with their footsteps from morning to night. On weekends he can be seen strapping on his  backpack and being towed away by his students for hiking and mountain climbing expeditions. He's tall, lean and fit and given to no visible vices save his usual after-meal cigarette. Inagaki is also a poet, and his *haiku* appears regularly in Japanese scholastic journals. He has had a lifelong interest in China, especially the twin provinces of Henan and Shanxi which he sees as the wellspring of Chinese culture from which Japanese culture derived. He reads Chinese, and even speaks a little. He also has limited—very limited—English. We converse about like this: "Inagaki go town today?" "Me . . . go . . . town . . . to . . . day . . . yes." You see, limited.

Inagaki is "laid back." Way laid back. I've never seen him in any way flustered, angry or exuberant. He is always in perfect control of himself. He keeps a suit in his apartment, and I've actually seen it on him a couple of times for formal occasions, but his habitual garb and classroom uniform is sneakers, jeans and assorted layers (depending on season) of shirts and sweaters culminating in his blue wind-breaker. His lank black hair is usually tussled. His eyebrows are small bushy triangles, and his habitual expression is one of weari-ness, pleasant weariness. He never gives offense. At the dining table he applies himself to his food, looks convivial, speaks seldom, and caps his meal with a leisurely cigarette—watching the wreaths of smoke coil upwards to the ceiling. Then he makes a quick, shallow bow from the waist, says "*zi jian*" ("goodbye"), and retires.

His sangfroid is admirable. During the course of our first con-versation together, when I learned he was living alone here but was married and had two adult sons, I asked, "Your . . . wife . . . home . . . in . . . Japan?" He replied, "Maybe." More recently at the dinner table, with Yumi interpreting, I asked Inagaki—well into his second year in China—if his wife missed him being gone so long. He re-sponded, "My wife thinks the husband who is healthy and not at home is the best husband. Many Japanese think so." With his chop-sticks he inserted a section of lotus into his mouth and chewed serenely.

Krishna Singh

I'm sitting on the couch doing nothing, thinking about noth-ing. My arms are spread out across the back of the couch. I'm pretty comfortable. I'm in control. In walks Krishna. I don't know how long it's been since Krishna stopped knocking and just began en-tering the apartment, but I guess long enough ago that it doesn't bother me anymore. He stands across the coffee table from me. He stares at me with those large liquid eyes—such an honest face really, such a good face, capped off by an eagle's beak of a nose. He's heard I'm currently writing about the Compound residents, and has a sheaf of papers in his hands which he presents to me in the formal

Chinese manner with both hands. I return the compliment, and accept with two hands. I sift through these papers, pretending to be interested. There are papers and certificates written in several languages—Nepalese, Hindi, English, Chinese—representing the way stations of his vagabond life. An Indian high school diploma, some sort of award for computer studies, a letter of acceptance to a medical school, a medical school to which his farmer parents back in Nepal with their few acres of rice paddies and five cows could never af-ford to send him. So he keeps the letter. There's a badly written traveller's brochure introducing Nepal: "For the nature lovers Nepal is such a land of natural beauty that metaphors cannot delineate its real picture. At the same time, Nepal proffers an incomparable scope to the connoisseurs of art and culture. . . ." On the brochure's map of Nepal an arrow points to an empty green area an inch east of Katmandu. Here Krishna has penned in the words "Babhangama Katti, Ward Number 5." He says, "Dees ees my village. Dees ees where my fodder's farm ees." "Do you think my readers will be wanting to know that you're from Ward Number 5 Krishna?" While he considers this, I let this stuff dribble out of my hands onto the coffee table. I don't know what kind of a book he thinks I'm writing or who he thinks needs to know about his slender achievements, but I'm reminded of that great Bogey line in "Casablanca": "I was misinformed." Krishna stands there before me: misinformed.

The clock is ticking towards midnight, December 31, 1999. It's Millenium Night! I'm seated in a canvas camp chair with two rope-handled ammunition boxes stacked beside me. Atop the ammo boxes rests my beer glass which a soldier keeps refilling. We're in an underground bunker of the Capital Defense Perimeter, and the male and female soldiers of the People's Liberation Army bunkered here are guarding Beijing's northern approaches. The Russian frontier is 300 road miles due north. But the Russians are not coming this night, and the new millenium is. So the soldiers have set about enjoying themselves. Beneath the camouflage netting, with moss dripping through the net gaps, a space has been cleared, candles have been lit, speakers and strobe lights hooked up. The young soldiers—and some civilian guests—now dance. The female soldiers are especially lovely: mottled green camouflage skirts, starched khaki blouses with shoulder tabs, scarlet ties. In the stuffy, overheated atmosphere they disco dance, spin all about, their silken hair and red ties lash this way and that. Their faces gleam in the candlelight and perspiration stains begin to ring their underarms. The young soldiers now form into a circle with their civilian guests—my wife, daughters and Krishna amongst them—and dance and clap in rhythm. One by one, people are coaxed into the middle for a solo stint. Now it's Krishna's turn. Roselyn comes out, Krishna goes in. Kirstin pulls him from the front, Helen pushes him from behind. He's in. *"Wo de tian! Wo de tian!"* ["Oh my God! Oh my God!"] He goes to work with a will. He hops and jerks about in that semi-coordinated gawky way of his—his head and shoulders towering above the others. The pulsating strobe light fixes his every posture, his every profile, for a millisecond. Arms this way and that; legs this way and that. Head down, beak down. Head up, beak up. *"Wo de tian! Wo de tian!"* Smiling, laughing. The high-pitched Krishna giggle. *"Wo de tian!"* He's happy. Happy.

"Is this for *real?*" you ask. Well, no. Actually, it's not. Oh, the dancing and Krishna's happiness are real enough, but almost everything else is bogus. This is not a *real* PLA bunker, but a small and very upscale nightclub in northern Beijing got up to look like a real PLA bunker. The boy and girl soldiers are not *real* soldiers, but graduates of the Chinese government's tourism schools got up to look like real soldiers and who have been trained to mix it up with the clientele when not engaged in other chores: bartending, waiting tables, hostessing. A soldier plonks a cocktail down on your ammo box, then invites you to dance with her (or him). It's all a lot of fun, and it's all very expensive. My bar tab will be huge.

When we first arrived in Xinxiang, Krishna was already a fixture of the Compound. He was starting his fourth year on the campus, studying computer engineering, and although he didn't live in the Compound per se, but in the cheaper hotel/dormitory immediately adjacent, he had earned the privilege of eating in our dining room by dent of his proficiency in six languages (Nepalese, Hindi, Urdu, English, Japanese and Chinese) and his knowledge of "the ropes" around the Compound, campus and city. He was invaluable in helping the *waiban* to "break in" new foreign teachers and students, particularly the annual contingent of Nepalese students whom he serves as *dai* ("elder brother") and interprets for until they acquire Chinese.

Krishna also earned himself a choice fourth-floor dormitory room with heat, carpeting, efficiency fridge, hot plate and rice cooker. This room he's made homey with wall posters, photos of parents, friends and dogs (which he adores), and little gifts and doo-dads which he has acquired during the course of his stay. Everything he owns is kept meticulously neat and clean. He has a weekly wipedown—not just a surface dusting—of all his possessions, and a sign on his door warns visitors to remove their shoes before entering his room. His non-perishable food-stuffs are displayed on shelves in descending order of box or bottle size with their labels carefully turned outwards for easy identification. That way you know just what you've got. If you get an invitation to dine with him in his room, as Roselyn, Helen and I frequently do, he'll be ready: a clothed table will have been placed in the room with four chairs and stools of assorted heights arranged about it, the table laid with unmatched plates and bowls, candles lit, soft sitar music will be emitting from the tape player.

Krishna's a perfect host: ladling out your individual portions of rice and curried mutton, fussing about, pouring you fragrant Nepalese teas. "What you think? You like? Ees good?" Often he'll propose a prayer before dining. He's a converted Christian. There is a crucifix that takes pride of place on the wall. The three of us, Roselyn, Helen, and I, were with him when he bought that crucifix. It was during an overnight stay we had in Kaifeng. Krishna spied the cross in a curio shop and decided he wanted it. No sooner had he completed that purchase than he spotted a brass knuckle-duster that had four brass spikes forged to the knuckle plate. He slid this wicked looking thing onto his hand, made a couple of practice jabs in the air with it, tapped it against his own chest, pondering the injury this weapon would inflict, and decided he needed to have it too. We all complimented him on his choice of purchases: "Nice combo Krishna," but the irony seemed to have escaped him. He even had the gall to use the strength of his crucifix purchase as grounds to beat the shopkeeper down on the price of his knuckle-duster purchase.

Actually, Krishna is an excellent bargainer, and we have used either his services or Helen's in that role throughout our stay in China. Their techniques are completely different. Helen relies on charm and flattery: these are poor foreign teachers; it is your duty to give them a good impression of China by offering them a fair price; I can see right away that you are a good and decent man. Krishna's technique is also simple, but requires iron nerves and a touch of callousness. The basic approach is to make the shopkeeper feel like he's a crook and his goods are trash. Okay, you need an abacus. You slip Krishna the money in small bills (this is crucial because in his method of bargaining it's too dangerous to stick around for change) and he goes over to take a look. The shopkeeper has one and takes it off the shelf and places it on the counter. It's a real beauty with brass hardware and nifty mahogany frame and counting beads. Krishna sneers at it and examines it six ways from Sunday looking for some defect, any defect. In this case there's a joint he finds a little weak, especially after he works on it a bit; also there is a tiny burr in one of the mahogany beads. He'll ask the shopkeeper how much he wants for this piece of rubbish, and all the while his finger keeps returning to that burr as if it were a scab. Eventually, he'll offer a brutally low price that'll practically choke the shopkeeper, but bargaining has begun, and Krishna will fight tenaciously for every yuan. When he knows he's close to, but still below, the shopkeeper's absolute bottom line, Krishna's mouth will go really mean and ugly, like he's just burped up a gob of bile, and he'll throw a wad of bills on the counter—like he's bitter over how badly this swindler has bamboozled him—grab the abacus and head for the door. Unless the shopkeeper actually flys out the door after him, physically wrestles the goods away from him, as they sometimes do, Krishna is away and clear. Around the corner he starts giggling that high-pitched Krishna giggle. *"Wo de tian! Wo de tian!"*

In addition to being our bargainer, Krishna serves as our medical consultant. He has a wealth of Nepalese folk adages. Some gems: walking barefoot on grass will improve your eyesight; eating eggplant will give you scabies; sweeping the dirt out of your house before daylight is bad, but don't ask Krishna why this is so, because "Ees secret."

By now you have probably formed the impression that Krishna is quite "a character." That is true, he is "a character," a person of unusual, even peculiar, personality. But he is also a man *of* character in the best sense of the word. He has real substance. And here let me say something about that nose of his: I believe it's his greatest feature. A godsend. Without it he would have been too perfect, absurdly handsome, a "pretty boy," and faced all the risks of vanity and shallowness such looks entail. That nose has made Krishna self-conscious and shaped both his physical and emotional character. It has made him sensitive, and he emanates sensitivity. I've met few people as aware of and sympathetic to their fellow man. From the time he gets up in the morning to the time he goes to bed at night he is involved in making life better for those around him. He bursts into the dining room at every meal with his *"ni hao folks"* or *"wo de tian,"* conscious of everyone's obligation to present at least a façade of cheerfullness in everyday life. He boosts morale. He remembers everyone's birthday, everyone's national day, and is constantly penning cards and letters to his many friends. He is never too busy to help language-challenged foreign teachers and students with shopping, train tickets, banking or doctors. He also offers wise counsel to those who care to seek it. In one instance I recall, a girl on the verge of graduation was in our living room speaking to Roselyn, Krishna and me. The girl was in tears—torn by her ambition to leave the province and seek her future elsewhere and her parents' insistence that she remain at home with them. After Roselyn and I said our piece, Krishna was asked his thoughts on the matter. He replied, "Parents leeve dere lifes. Dees ees your life. You leeve your life." The girl followed his advice.

Krishna also has strict moral standards. Consequently, watching movies with him on a VCR is always a disjointed affair. Even such mildly risque fare as "The Bridges of Madison County" or "The Joy Luck Club" are sure to meet with his disapproval. At the first sign of a button being unbuttoned Krishna acts. "Stop. STOP!" he shouts. "We are here. We are watching. Dees ees bad. BAD!" And he's not kidding. He'll turn off the screen and fast forward to safer ground. Any depiction of sex disturbs him, and premarital and extramarital sex are anathema. He, a 24-year-old man, has frequently said he is determined to have sex with only one woman during his life: the woman he eventually marries. As *dai,* "elder brother," to the campus Nepalese contingent he feels responsible, rightly or wrongly, for any misbehavior on their part. He'll take them to task anytime one of them "shames" their country by getting drunk (as some of them do) or dances in a manner he considers lewd (as some of them do). He'll yell at them; he'll threaten to report them to the *waiban* or even to write their parents back in Nepal. Although he rarely does this, and will usually forgive them after a few days, (he is, after all, a Christian), his anger and disappointment are quite genuine. And, pushed hard enough, he does act, and will then dispatch an admirably blunt letter like this one:

> Dear Parents,
>   We feel very embarrased to inform you that your son is doing nothing over here. He is just wasting time, money and energy. He never attends classes. He is always organizing parties, drinking beer and wine and making a lot of noise after midnight. We have tried our best to help him to improve but we have lost hope. We are just tired.
>   So, we kindly request that you write to your son and give him some good advice. We will be very sorry if we have to send him back to Nepal.
>   We hope you will understand our intentions.
> Yours faithfully,
>
> Krishna Singh
> Foreign Affairs Office
> Henan Normal University

It's one o'clock on a cold February night. I'm seated on a stool drawn up beside Krishna's bed in a Xinxiang hospital. An impacted wisdom tooth has "blown up" on him, leading to an emergency visit to the hospital. The doctors have had him on a saline drip for the better part of the evening, trying to contain the pain and swelling. Krishna, who has never before in his life had an injection, let alone a shunt run up his arm, has been traumatized by the night's events. He lays immobilized by pain and is tethered to a drip stand in the shabby ward. His eyes are awash with suffering, and every time he blinks, his eyes threaten to roll up into his head like a doll's. I try to comfort him: "You know, Krishna, the funny thing about pain is that no one else feels it. Here we are, your head a foot away from mine, yours bursting with pain, and I don't feel a thing. Actually, I feel pretty good."

"Beel. You bad boy."

"And my teeth . . . my teeth feel terrific." I snap them hard three times to demonstrate: "Click! Click! Click!"

"Velly, velly bad."

But what bothers Krishna the most is that the Nepalese students haven't come to see him. He moans: "Why dey not come? Why dey not here? I luke after dem. I take care dem. I take dem hospital. Dey my brudders. Why dey forget Krishna? [Long pause.] I hope dey die."

Back in his dorm two days later he tapes a sign on his door: "Go away. I am dead."

Three days later he removes it.

Krishna, our dear friend.

The University

The university proper is reached at the eastern end of Xinxiang's Jianshe Road, an arterial road running right across the northern section of the city, and a road so dense with buses, bicycles, trishaws and pony carts that all traffic creeps along at pedestrian pace. Once one pushes past the hawkers, market carts and sidewalk booksellers of the teeming, trash-strewn street, one arrives at the maroon, marble-slabbed main gate which bears brass characters proclaiming the universtiy's motto: "Unity, Diligence, Realism, Creativity." Just walk on by the four or five gate guards in their slovenly, green, army-style uniforms who sprawl in wire and wicker chairs and scrutinize with lazy insolence everyone who enters or leaves this walled enclave—this walled city.

The first thing you will notice, once inside, is a 20-foot-tall granite Mao standing atop a pedestal. He stands serene and smug, with a hint of a smile, possibly unaware of his waning popularity in the more modern, cynical metropolises of coastal China. His right arm is raised in benign benediction and every afternoon and weekend, summer or winter, spring or fall, unprosperous looking photographers jostle about with cameras and tripods snapping students, visiting peasant parents, stamp clubs and soccer teams beneath that benedictory arm. Some of the photographic subjects will

wear a smile, but most apparently feel a serious scowl more be-
hooving. Some noble poses are struck.

Beyond Mao lies the campus. The broad entry road bifurcates
before his pedestal and bifurcates again and again beyond him:
streets become alleys, alleys become *hutongs* barely wide enough for
two bikes to pass abreast. You begin to appreciate the density of
population within this educational city within a city. Twenty thousand people not only work and study here, but live here, within the
walls of these 110 scant acres.

Aside from the dozens of classroom buildings are 43 mainly
six-story apartment blocks, rank after rank of them, that house the
1700 faculty members, plus their families (spouses, children, aunts,
aged parents, what have you) and thousands of others: administrators, secretaries, maintenance workers, cleaners, groundkeepers,
guards, cooks, hotel workers, nurses, street sweepers, laboratory
technicians, librarians, steam plant operators. Then there are the
factory workers for the four university-owned factories within the
walls: a yogurt factory, a microscope slide factory, a bookbindery,
the Yulin basketball and soccer ball factory. And then there are the
legions of faculty, staff and factory workers who have been shoved
into an early retirement (60 for males, 55 for women) to make way
for younger employees. These elderly, and not so elderly, folks pot-
ter about the place, stay out of the way as much as possible, and po-
litely wait for the conveyor belt of life to carry them off to obliv-
ion. Altogether, 10,000 people dwell in the 43 faculty and staff
apartment blocks.

And, finally, there are the 10,000 resident students. But
whereas 43 apartment blocks are needed to house the 10,000 faculty
and staff family members, just nine similarly-sized dormitory
blocks suffice for the 10,000 students. How is this possible you may
wonder? Well, the answer is easy. The students are packed in—
packed in tight. They live in dormitory rooms 16 feet long by 10
feet wide (160 square feet), eight students to a room. That works
out to 20 square feet per person. Imagine it! Mark off a square four-
and-a-half feet by four-and-a-half feet on the floor. Now stand inside it. Okay, that's your share of the room. No judge in America
would tolerate for an instant such cramped living conditions in an
American prison. But these are not American prisoners luxuriating
in their roomy cells. These are Chinese students, and they do accept

the spartan conditions. In their dorm rooms two double-decker beds line each side of the room and a long, narrow desk occupies the space between. Stools, not chairs, but backless stools, are tucked beneath the desk and may be pulled out for use. On either side of the entry door are small cupboards stacked four high where each of the eight residents may lock their few possessions: spare clothes, books, ping-pong paddles, and so forth. Another small cabinet in the room is fitted with eight racks for students to store their plastic wash basins. The dorm window opens outward to give access to two arm-breadth-long wires strung between two stanchions: the clothesline for the room's occupants. The floor is bare concrete. The room is unheated.

Now picture the life here. Let's take the wee hours of a January night. The thermometer stands at 15 degrees Farenheit—17 degrees of frost obtain—and snow is banked upon the ground. A steady 20 mile-per-hour wind is coming in from across the Gobi, coming in from Siberia. The northern faces of the 4- and 6-storied dormitory blocks take the brunt. The windows' thin panes rattle; cracked and broken panes admit the chilled, unbelievably dry air. Sheets and other makeshift curtains the students have nailed to the windows billow in the wind. A wash basin negligently left overnight on the desk glazes over in the drafty room. The room, like the entire building, is dark. Black dark. All electricity to the dorms is shut down from 11:00 to 4:00 each night. But there are a thousand human beings in this building and there is some movement by aid of flashlight. Nature calls, and a cone of light emerges from behind a closed door and probes the corridor. The patter of feet. Then silence. The girls—and, this being a normal school, 80 percent of the students are girls—lie under their quilts in fetal positions wearing double layers of socks and thermal underwear and often their coats as well. In many bunks two or three girls cling together to share body heat. Somehow another night passes.

At 4:00 A.M. the dorms power back up. Girls begin to climb down from their bunks onto the concrete floor. In slippers they shuffle off towards the toilets, guided by the odor as much as anything. The 200-plus girls on each floor share two facilities at either end of the corridor—each having eight open squat toilets. The business is quickly done. Many girls hold their breath and close their eyes while in the room because of the acrid stench and burning ammonia. Once they leave, their clothes and hair will hint gently of urine and excrement for half the morning. They then make their way to the "water room." In the water room a pipe bearing near-freezing water is suspended over a long, waist-high trough. Eight spigots along the pipe can be ducked under to dowse heads, but most girls draw a basin of frigid water and return to the relative privacy of their dormrooms to wash faces, private parts and feet in that order. They chew toothpaste and spit it into the basin. The wastewater is tossed out. Also, in most rooms, the girls rotate the unpleasant duty of one of them carrying thermoses to the "hot water place," a shed beside the coal-fired steam plant where steam-heated exhaust water can be drawn from another pipe suspended over another long trough. Lines of thermos-laden students stand in a fog of steam waiting turns at one of the multiple spigots. Back at the dorms this water will be transferred into smaller hot water flasks that each student will carry about during the day and which will fulfill multiple roles: drinking water, tea water, hand warmer.

The girls now "bundle up"—add on more layers of clothing over their double layers of thermal underwear top and bottom. Two pairs of tight-fitting pants; two or three sweaters. Then the coats, hoods, scarves and mittens. Thin girls become medium-sized girls, medium-sized girls become fat girls. Fortunately, the sequence ends there for there is not a single, truly fat girl on campus—stringent, mandatory, "must pass," annual physical fitness testing accounts for that and also accounts for there being no physically handicapped students on campus (they are shunted off to "special" schools), except for a single, powerfully-built, one-armed male, who is the reigning All-China Shot-Put Champion.

But to continue, the hooded or hatted, scarved and mittened girls trail off now on foot or bikes (if surface conditions permit) for the library or classrooms. By 5:00 A.M. the library and every classroom building on campus are ablaze with lights from top to bottom. The students inside have their heads down studying even though it will be another three hours before their first professors arrive. I must say, the campus at this time is impressive. It makes you proud. Those blazing towers of light. Those splendid young people. You can't help but admire them. They work so hard; they live so hard; and they never complain. Thank God they are mainly the sons and daughters of peasants. Who else would be tough enough to not only accept such a life, but to actually embrace it? Most of them think they've "got it good," and they do compared to their peasant parents. To them life has handed them an almost unimaginable opportunity (only three percent of China's young people—the cream of their youth—are selected for university education), and they won't let that opportunity slip them by. It's impossible not to make some comparisons—some very unfavorable comparisons—between what these Chinese students are doing at 5:00 A.M. and what their American counterparts are doing at that same hour—perhaps blundering back to their plush dorm rooms and fraternity houses after a hard night of keg parties and panty raids. But I suppose it's probably unwise to pursue such comparisons further. The systems are just so different—as any day at Henan Normal would prove.

At 5:50 A.M., the dorm monitors, all members of the Communist Youth League, and answerable to the powerful Student Union's Disciplinary Committee, begin moving through the dorms with police whistles to drive out the laggards. Anyone caught inside the buildings after formal reveille at 6:00 A.M. will be punished (usually public criticism and fines for initial offenders). Once reveille (blown on a bugle and amplified all over campus by the ubiquitous loudspeakers—to accompany the color detail's flag hoisting at flag square) is complete at 6:10, the dorms are closed to all but the members of the cleaning details. One rotatable person appointed by each dorm room's monitor stays behind to clean the room and prepare it for inspection: beds made, clothes folded and put away, floors swept and mopped, trash emptied. A rather cursory inspection takes place daily, a more serious, graded inspection is made weekly, and dreaded surprise inspections may come at anytime night or day. The main purpose of the surprise inspections is to ferret out contraband and punish malefactors. Contraband includes, among other things, any heating device, any cooking device or utensil, any candle, any television set. (A handful of students who have obtained a special license and are able to pay a hefty electrical fee are authorized to keep small televisions.)

The classroom routine at Henan Normal, as at most other universities in China, would also amaze Westerners. The students, except for the privileged seniors, move through their day in lockstep. There is minimal freedom. To begin with, there is no free and easy selecting of this course or that course, no dabbling with an elective here and an elective there. And certainly there's no switching of majors. There is no nonsense of any kind like that. High school graduates who manage to pass the drastically competitive NMET (National Matriculation Entrance Test) are admitted into a university and join a year group (say, 1998 inductees) where they are lumped together by major, and then assigned to a specific class, for example, "1998 English Majors, Class Five." The students of this class then form a cohesive body as tight as any army platoon. They are bunked together in the same dorms and processed through the system as a body in four years time—not more, not less. For the most part they will sit in their class's individual "classroom," seated in the same two-person desk, with the same "deskmate," all day long, and different professors will be cycled in to instruct them.

The students do not receive a broad-based education as students do in America. There is no effort to make Chinese students "well-rounded." They are narrowly educated to achieve expertise in their major field. Here, for instance, is the hefty, 22-hour class load for all sophomore English majors in their first semester: Intensive Reading of English—6 hours; Extensive Reading of English—2 hours; English Listening—4 hours; English Writing—2 hours; English Grammar—2 hours; Oral English—2 hours; Marxism—2 hours; Physical Education—2 hours. Every semester, every year is just as finely focused. The strengths of such an educational system are obvious, and the weaknesses of such an educational system are just as obvious, although, I suppose it should be said, the weaknesses are somewhat ameliorated by the fact that all the university students have the benefit of their superb high school training wherein they did receive broad-based education in mathematics, sciences, literature, and social and historical topics—albeit with a deep, deep communist bias.

And that communist bias, incidentally, persists into university and dampens free thought and creativity in every class. It's oppressive. Here's me arriving for a sophomore English Writing class. Just east of the Mao statue I enter Number One Building—home of the English Department—a four-story, half-block-long edifice of gray-brown brick the Russians designed and helped erect back during the Sino-Soviet honeymoon period of the Fifties. The sweep of the cavernous entry hall is broken by concrete pillars supporting the floor above. The entry hall is unlit except for the faint daylight seeping in from the entry doors. The walls are scabrous. Decades ago they were painted half way up in institutional green—white above—but over the years most of the paint has sluffed away, and the rest is going. Posters in Chinese characters announcing this exam result or that, this special lecture or that, get pasted up, peeled down, or are just left to hang in shreds. The bare concrete floor is everywhere pitted and cratered. Two single-axled, spoke-wheeled, man-pulled trash carts are parked in the entry hall. The pullers will be somewhere in the building dragging large cardboard boxes through the corridors gathering up trash. In a little room opening off of the entryhall sits the building's caretaker. He is a man of considerable antiquity with few teeth. He is watching TV and sucking up a bowl of noodles. He wears a white cotton surgeon's cap with strings that tie up under his chin. I walk past the department's office. (This is easy to identify because there is a hand-painted wooden sign affixed beside the door. The sign says: "Department of English." The letters are none of them of the same thickness nor height, and they tend to trail off lower and lower on the board as you move to the right. Inside the office are some gym lockers which house the department's files, four wooden desks which were apparently part of the building's original furnishings, a few assorted chairs, and a sofa to rest upon that's missing its cushions. Bare concrete floor of course.) I go up the east stairway. I go carefully. A half-century's worth of student feet has eroded and crumbled the stair ridges and climbing is tricky. At the second floor landing a discarded sofa permanently rests with the cushions missing and its back and sides split open and leaking cotton. I keep going up. On the third floor I turn left and proceed down a long corridor. This is a corridor of which my daughter, when first she looked down it, remarked: "Oh my God! If you started crying you could never stop." The corridor is unlit except for the light afforded by the narrow windows at its two distant ends. The bare concrete floor here is in an advanced stage of disintegration. Not only is it pitted and cratered, but it also has areas where whole layers of concrete have cracked loose in slabs and been carted off. The classrooms are to either side of the corridor. The rooms are numbered, but it is difficult to read the numbers. Some rooms have numbers painted on their doors with the use of a child's stencil set, some have numbers written with a magic marker, some have numbers scrawled across the door in chalk. Each door has a hasp, thick chain and padlock. (The padlock key will be owned by the class's "monitor," invariably an energetic, capable and ambitious member of the Communist Youth League, and not by any professor.) The room's door, door jamb and immediate adjacent wall area are stained to a rich, deep brown by the accumulated hand grease of generations of students. This filth is never cleaned, never painted over. The padlock is off. The chain—thick as a car tow-chain—hangs loose. I push on the door. You always half-doubt the class will be in there. There's never any noise. But they always *are* in there, quiet, quiet as mice, studying or resting their heads on their desks—waiting for their next professor. They're packed in tight, really, really tight. They have tiny two-person desks and stools with a seat area the size of a sheet of notebook paper. They are seated so closely that if anyone stands or moves a half-dozen people are inconvenienced. There are 34 students in a 300-square foot room. I step to the speaker's platform. I ask the monitor if everyone is present. The monitor, in this case a female, stands and points to one empty stool. "That girl's family has trouble and she got leave to go home on the train last night." Okay, so I begin. I tell them we're going to write a three paragraph, timed essay of 35 minutes to begin the class. I write the topic on the blackboard: "If Taiwan proclaims independence, China should invade Taiwan." I tell the students on the right-hand side of the room to write in favor of the proposition; those on the left-hand side to write in opposition to the proposition. Immediately the monitor stands up: "This topic is not suitable. We shouldn't write about it."

"Why isn't it suitable?"

"It's political."

"I know it's political, and I think it is suitable. It's a topic that's been at the top of the news all week and we all know something about it."

The monitor's deskmate now stands and adds her thoughts on the matter: "If you make us write about this we will stop liking you."

The monitor, still standing, leafs rapidly back and forth through the pages of her Chinese-English dictionary. She then says, "'Invade.' We cannot use that word. Taiwan is part of China. So we cannot 'invade' our own country."

"Well then, what word *can* we use? We all know what we mean."

Other students are now also murmuring and leafing through their dictionaries. Different words are proposed. Finally we settle on this wording: "If Taiwan declares independence, China should use force to recover Taiwan."

Thirty minutes later the essays are written and I leave the platform and take the empty stool of the absent girl. I call for volunteers to go to the platform and read their essays. Without further prompting one after another of the students from the "pro" side of the room proceeds to the platform and reads out a blistering speech in favor of "using force." They all know the platform procession format well because it is the same routine used at their bi-weekly Communist Youth League meetings wherein budding and ambitious young communists can earn brownie points with the department's Party leaders. So now, they are all trooping down trying to out-do one another in trumpeting the official Party line. Again and again, they parrot the words that the Taiwanese problem is an "internal issue" and that foreigners have "no right to interfere." One girl in the class whom I've never really hit it off with—I don't know why for sure, but I think there has always been something in her manner towards me that signals that she really does regard me as a "foreign devil"—delivers an ugly, xenophobic diatribe while her eyes flicker venom at me. She wins a big round of applause and flounces back to her seat. Just before she sits down, she turns her head and, cool as you please, stares hard at me.

Up to this point, I've been maintaining a calm, completely professional demeanor, as if not a word or look has phased me in the least, but, I must admit, this is beginning to be an effort. Inwardly, I'm feeling very uncomfortable. I've spent a lot of time and thought in gaining good rapport with my students. We've always been on the friendliest terms. I know every one of these kids; they are frequent guests in my home; some of them, for God's sake, I've been helping out financially. I don't want all this mutual goodwill to evaporate in the course of an afternoon.

So far no one from the "con" side of the room has stirred a muscle. They all sit on their stools looking down at their desks. They don't want to make eye contact with me for fear they'll be called to the platform. But, finally, one girl on the "con" side stands and proceeds to the platform. Every eye is upon her. And what does she do? She announces that she refuses to argue as "Mr. Bill" has directed, and she's gung ho for using force too. Her defection earns her a hearty round of applause. But just when I'm about to despair, one of the classroom's quietest, shyest girls moves to the platform and begins to read from her paper. Without once looking up, and in a barely audible voice, she delivers an intelligent speech, arguing for "patience," arguing against "brothers killing brothers," arguing that a conflict with Taiwan could be devastating to the economies of both lands. This brave little soul then folds up her paper, says, "That's all," and returns to her stool. She gets no applause, and my praise for her has to be limited to "nicely reasoned" and "well argued" for fear my current unpopularity rubs off on her.

It's now time for my homework assignment, and here I make a lightning adjustment. Instead of having them write an essay on "China's Use of Capital Punishment" as I had planned, I come up with this milksop: "What Friendship Means to Me." Everyone seems happy.

Pretty feeble. I know. But I too, like everyone else in China, am to some degree intimidated by the system. As a foreign teacher I may have less to lose than most, certainly less than my students, but I cannot criticize with impunity. There's more at stake than just premature ejection from the country for me and my wife. There's Helen and her family to consider. Any official displeasure with me could have repercussions on her and them. And what, after all, would I accomplish with ineffectual classroom sniping at the Party, human rights, Taiwan? Nothing or next to nothing. I know there is disaffection with the Party, with the authoritarianism, with corruption in China, but it is difficult to judge how intense or widespread it is. I'm almost positive that it is nowhere near achieving a critical mass. Undoubtedly there are some driven individuals out there working for the day when they can disrupt the inertia of the "system," but most people, most of my students, are just scuttling around trying to accommodate themselves to life as they find it, looking out for themselves and their families, getting what happiness they can.

Moreover, my students, irregardless of their political views, have an abiding love for China—the land of China. Their allegiance resonates throughout their essays which are filled with testimonials of their loyalty to the "motherland." Helen, for instance, writes:

I'm a very patriotic person. I love my country deeply. Whether rich or poor, advanced or backward, it is always the most beautiful land in my mind. I'm a small leaf on the tree and my country is the root. Since I'm getting my nutrients from her, there is no reason I'm not grateful or thankful to her. I'm determined to devote myself to the development and prosperity of her.

This patriotism is most evident in the students' overwhelmingly favorable responses to their month of mandatory military training which comes in their sophomore year and is a prerequisite for acquiring a university degree in China. When the drill instructors arrived at Henan Normal University, having marched all the way from their base at Baiguan, the 2,000 sophomore trainees (mainly girls remember) were initially traumatized by the ferocity—the intentional ferocity—of the experience. They wept as their precious pigtails were mercilessly lopped off; they cringed when forced to don ill-fitting, baggy, green fatigues which they all claimed made them look fat (but which didn't); and they sweated like beasts when they were forced to stand absolutely motionless in the August sun with playing cards clamped between their knees. A half hour. An hour. A single card drops and all are punished by starting the clock again. After three days of repeating orders by bellowing them out at the top of their lungs, many girls had throats swollen up like frogs.

But the students, being of basically peasant stock, were naturally resilient and adaptable: they all learned to march; they all learned to shoot; and they all learned elementary battlefield tactics. Their skin grew dark. They got used to plowing through mud on their bellies with rifles cradled in the crooks of their arms. And they also got used to and delighted in the camaraderie of sitting cross-legged in circles at night and hearing "real army stories" from the mouths of their now relaxed instructors, and being taught army songs, patriot songs. Here, probably more than anywhere else, the Government was realizing its stated goal: "to cultivate (in the students) a sense of responsibility for our nation." That goal was met at Henan Normal University. When, after a month, the instructors boarded trucks to return to base, the student trainees, now "veterans," mobbed them at the school gate, pelted them with flowers and there was much mutual saluting and shedding of tears. "Long live the soldiers!" Students' fists upraised. "Long live the students!" Soldiers' fists upraised.

Such scenes as this go far to illustrate just how far apart Chinese society is from Western society or, for that matter, almost any other society. Perhaps only North Korea's universities would be as narrowly focused and militarized as China's. But educational reform is coming to China, if slowly. When I first arrived at the university and was asked to sit down with the department's Party chieftains, "the leaders" as they are always called, of the 72-faculty member English Department, they did unexpectedly encourage me to introduce some "modern Western methods" in my classrooms: invite debate, assign stimulating essays, reward creativity, and break with the Chinese educational mainstay of strict "rote" learning. But despite my limited ventures into those styles of teaching, it became quickly apparent to me that it was rote learning that my students were most used to, most comfortable with, and which they most excelled at—excelled at amazingly well. This I discovered to my discomfiture at the close of my first semester at HNU when I graded the exams of my 130-student American History class. I made the mistake of administering the same examination paper I was used to giving my American students back at the University of Texas in Brownsville. But whereas in Texas that exam paper always rendered me a nice spread of As, Bs, Cs, Ds, and Fs, here in China I ended up with 90 percent As. Oh, my Chinese students loved their "Mr. Bill" all right, but the department leaders decided my course was a joke—and made me promise to absolutely crucify my students in the next semester to make up for it. Obviously those "towers of light" ablaze around the campus at 5 A.M. are not "ablaze" for nothing.

But it would be erroneous to think that Chinese college students have no fun. They do, the classmates and dormmates share the joys of a deep camaraderie such as only small, tight military units enjoy. They live together, struggle together, share together. They look out for each other. For instance, amongst the 160 Year 2 English majors which I teach, 14 have been identified by the class tutor and monitors as suffering "acute poverty," that is, being the sons and daughters of peasants with extremely small farm plots, and often with the father dead. To assist these 14, the other members of the class voluntarily tax themselves two yuan (24 cents) a month. Moreover, the eight dormmates of a dorm unit will often "carry" one of their impoverished members at meal times by allowing that hungry "eighth" two pokes of the chopsticks from each of their seven bowls. And, as far as I can observe, this is always done unresentfully even though the other seven are usually only marginally better off.

And the students share clothes too. Most of them have very few clothes. This is one of the reasons it is easy for me to remember students' names. I have not only their faces to go by, but also their clothes: green sweater girl, bib-overalls girls, uniform boy—a boy who wears the same second-hand, woolen, army surplus uniform season round. But if a girl gets asked by a boy to meet him at the campus park on the weekend, to walk with a boy outside the gate for an ice cream cone, the girls of the dorm unit will all pitch in to clothe that girl adequately—make sure she looks new and fresh.

"Shower Time" is another happy time for students. On the weekends they'll file off in groups for their weekly shower at one of the two campus bath-houses: boys with boys, and the far more numerous girls with other girls. They'll pay their one yuan (12 cents), enter the change room, strip naked, undo their braids, and then pile into the steamy shower room a hundred or more at a time and scramble for spray space beneath the two dozen showerheads. As chirpy as sparrows in the rain, they'll be hopping in and out from under the sprinklers, shampooing and rinsing hair, lathering up, and then, with the assistance of their "back mates," unabashedly scrubbing each other down.

The kids like playing too. And that's what they call it: "playing." It makes them sound so innocent, and in many ways they are. They'll ask each other out to "play" during "playtime," which is from 4 o'clock to 6 o'clock in the afternoon—the only time in the day when they are not in the classroom or engaged in study. On the two large playing fields which can accommodate a few thousand students at a time, there are courts for soccer, basketball, volleyball and badminton. But the most popular sport of all—a permanent craze—is ping-pong. It's enjoyed by nearly everyone: students and faculty members, both sexes. There are ping-pong halls dotted all around the campus, and permanent, concrete tables have been constructed here, there and everywhere. In the classroom blocks themselves I'd estimate every tenth room has been converted into a ping-pong room. Each department's faculty members have their own exclusive ping-pong room. Our big English Department has several such rooms and between classes you'll see instructors—men and women, all ages—in there slamming away at each other. Giggling. It's good relaxation.

The students, same as their countrymen everywhere, also like playing cards—all kinds of cards. One card game, the stupidest I've ever seen, is a favorite among the girls on campus and is used to predict what their future husbands will be like. This game was demonstrated to me by the campus "master," one of my senior students named Yang Hua Jing ("Jane"). The game is both complicated and assinine. It passes through several ridiculous stages wherein the number of suitors a girl will have is finally deciphered, and then the rival suitors eliminate one another until one—"*the* one"—emerges triumphant. The game then proceeds to its final stage, its most consequential stage, its "moment of truth" so to speak. Sixteen cards are flipped over and melded into suits. The strength of each suit is critical for suits represents one of the four characteristics Chinese girls consider of uppermost importance in selecting a husband: diamonds—wealth; spades—educational attainment; hearts—looks; clubs—height. Now *that* is interesting. Height outranks health, personality, family status, and so forth in this height-challenged land.

Jane is now initiating one of my sophomore girls into the mysteries of the game. The ultimate phase is reached. The 16 cards are flipped. *Voilà:* six diamonds, six spades, three hearts, one club. Jane soberly and softly informs the girl that she'll have a wealthy, well-educated, fairly ugly dwarf for a husband. The girl, the prospective bride, scrunches up her brow. Her slant eyes narrow and take on a faraway look as though she were trying to focus on that rich runt on the far horizon. She does not appear to be too happy.

To teach these students—these diligent, amiable, really rather lovable students—is a faculty mighty in numbers but weak in pay. Rookie instructors with masters degrees start at 500 yuan ($62) a month and cap out after about twenty years at 1100 yuan ($136). Holders of doctorates are only slightly better paid, but are better placed to jockey for leadership posts and other perks. Still, very few of my colleagues can aspire to my peak-of-the-pyramid 2200 yuan ($272) a month. In fact, several of my fellow professors, who discuss one another's salaries and overall financial situations as casually as Westerners discuss the weather, told me that only the university's president and the university's Party secretary pulled down more money than me.

Because of the pitiful pay—low even by Chinese standards—my colleagues have to scramble for every little bonus, every little scrap of money they can get, by performing extra duties. For instance, to supervise an end-of-year exam earns you 10 yuan ($1.22), directing a student's thesis, 20 yuan ($2.44). These sums might seem comical to American professors, but believe me I didn't feel like laughing when I lined up with my department colleagues for the end-of-semester bonus payouts and watched how eagerly each of them snatched up the pittance and double-checked that it was counted correctly.

The one saving grace for faculty financial fortunes is that they do not have to pay much for their campus housing. In fact, in the past, they only had to pay token rents of one to two dollars per month. Of course, with the nation's growing capitalism (called "New Socialism"—a figleaf euphemism coined to spare Communist Party embarrassment) everything is moving in the direction of privatization and faculty housing is no exception. Faculty members are now under pressure to buy their apartments or risk losing them. Luckily the apartments are being offered up at bargain basement prices: 6,000 yuan ($740) for a tiny flat in an older apartment block and ratcheting up to 70,000 yuan ($8,642) for a 3-bedroom heated flat in a newer block. Still, affording an $8,000+ flat on a hundred dollar a month salary is no mean feat, and professors are scrambling for loans from banks and/or their families. But when they succeed they find it difficult to disguise their pride. They are childishly anxious to show off their shiny new floors and open doors onto little bedrooms with a flourish. Inevitably an out-sized color TV will hulk in the cramped living room, still wearing its manufacturer's labels. The Chinese prize these labels. They are never removed. They are left on everything—refrigerators, fans, rice cookers, lamps, everything—to testify to the owner's financial well-being. (Incidentally, my male colleagues never remove the factory tags stitched to their suit cuffs and will flash these at you like money long after the garment has grown threadbare.) In fact, it would not be too strong to say the Chinese are enthralled with newness, with modernity. Like peoples crawling out of poverty all around the globe they are attracted by anything slick and shiny and have not had time yet to develop discriminating tastes. Browsing furniture stores they have an almost uncanny knack for honing in on the most hideous, tackiest pieces available—horrible, glitzy, aerodynamic stuff. And that's the junk they'll drag off to outfit their new apartments.

All right, so I'm being shown around still another of my colleagues' spanking new apartments. He is a learned man, a cultured man, and yet not even he "gets it." We are concluding the requisite apartment inspection. I wear the same old shockproof, fixed grin I always do as I am herded through one room after another. One last room to go. The best has been saved for last. I am conducted to a wall where my house-proud host's "treasure" hangs: a framed print. My host is watching me. I can feel him studying my face—eager for the approval of my Western eyes. The print bears a European motif. Some gentle folk of a bygone era wearing top hats and twirling parasols are riding in a horse-drawn carriage down a country lane. An ivy-shrouded, thatched cottage nestles in the background. Two well-bred setters with heads held high lope beside the carriage. My host fixes me with a "so-what-do-you-think-of-that" smile. The print is set off by a two-tone pink and gold tube frame. Delight is frozen on my face. I like my colleague. "Nice. Very Nice."

Workloads and working conditions for the faculty seem reasonable to me, at least on the surface. Most professors carry a standard 12-hour teaching load the same as their American counterparts, and the pressure to publish is probably no more intense than it is in the States. Certainly there is no "publish or perish" atmosphere, although books and journal articles are a prerequisite for promotions. On the other hand, I suspect office politics are far more intricate and vicious than in the States, although I have little concrete knowledge of specifics and am only surmising this from undertones. I am intentionally kept ignorant of such things by the department leaders. Both Adam and I are excluded from all administrative affairs. In a transparent ruse, we are the only two members of the 72-member-strong English Department assigned to instruct classes from 2 to 4 o'clock on Tuesday afternoons during which time the two-hour weekly departmental meetings are held. I do know the department's inner workings are of Byzantine complexity with deans, vice-deans, chairs and vice-chairs striving for authority with departmental Party secretaries who carry real clout. Most of the instructors are Party members themselves and obligated to follow the guidance of the secretaries. Nevertheless, there are exceptions. Able, competent Dr. Li Wenzhong is one non-Party member who still manages to hold down the position of vice-dean of the department through sheer competence and excellent people skills. I don't know if this would be possible in any other department as I get the impression that the university administrators tolerate more political and cultural unorthodoxy in the English Department than they do in the other university divisions. After all, in the English Department they are dealing with faculty members who have spent their entire adult lives studying an alien language and steeping themselves in the liberal themes of British and American literature. Such a faculty could not help but be somewhat "tainted" by Western ideals. Consequently, the administration grants them a little more leeway than they do teachers in the other disciplines. I liken the English faculty here to Fine Arts faculties in Western universities. You've got to expect and put up with a fair share of weirdos and wackos. It's the nature of the beast.

But even though the university leaders are apparently willing to endure some of the unorthodox shenanigans of the English Department misfits, it is truly a wonder how they manage to stomach our department's one true rogue elephant: a towering, shambling, raggedy wreck of an individual, the incomparable Mr. Lu Yuefeng. That this liberal, democratic Europhile has survived in this university is truly mystifying and must be indicative of *something*—perhaps that China really is changing. Had Mr. Lu been teaching back during the Cultural Revolution he would have been a dead man. No ands, ifs and buts about it. As it is his outspoken advocacy of democratic principles and his attendance at Tiananmen Square in 1989—*with some of his students in tow*—irrevocably blotted his record and froze up his career prospects. Barred from promotions, ineligible for pay raises and left in impoverishment, perhaps he serves as a useful reminder to others of the penalties entailed in trying to buck the system. But buck it he does. With impressive courage he lambasts communism, atheism, the Party, the whole Chinese "system" in lecture after lecture—lectures which are amongst the most popular on the campus with the students. Abandoned by society, ignored (but not despised) by his colleagues, he bravely plows ahead with his one-man campaign to vilify the system in his European Culture class and British and American Literature class. Under the guise of an understanding of Christianity being essential to understanding Western culture and literature, he openly reads from the Bible in class. Now that takes nerve! Even more provocatively he tells the students:

> You have been trained to be atheists, to be loyal to the Party. That's gibberish. Life begins in a garden and ends in a Bible. You don't believe me now, but wait and see. You'll know when you grow older that I am speaking the truth.

This raging individualist also hates conformity. Chain-smoking his way through another lecture—itself another infraction of the rules—he tells the students:

> Henan Normal University is a factory. We teachers are the machines; you students are the products; and you students will come out of this factory "normalized." If you are too much of an individual in this society, you will be persecuted. But try for a compromise. Try to be partly individualized, partly "normalized." The reality of this society is that to be a successful person you are going to have to be "normalized." But try to save what you can of your individualism.

I believe Mr. Lu is flirting with serious trouble. I've even heard some of the students express fear for him. Some have said they believe Mr. Lu is actually suicidal and feels he has nothing to lose. I don't know about that, but I do know I'd tip my hat to this man any day.

A Photo Essay of Xinxiang

Photographs by

William and Roselyn Adams

Downtown Xinxiang. The intersection of Pingyuan Road and Victory Road with a state-owned department store in the background. Private cars are still a rarity in China, but virtually anywhere in Xinxiang may be reached for about $1 in the ubiquitous "bread loaf" taxis seen here.

"The Poor Man's Paris." There are many beautiful tree-lined boulevards in Xinxiang. This is a stretch of the People's Road where the traffic testifies to the saying, "In China the bicycle is king." Here the bicycle lane is being casually infringed upon by pedestrians.

The power of the state. At 30 stories, "The People's Police Building" on Eastern Main Road is the tallest building in Xinxiang.

Hotel fronting onto Railroad Station Square. The signs inform detraining passengers of a variety of goods produced by Xinxiang factories: electric motors, machine tools, paper, coal mining equipment.

A shopping district along Pingyuan Road. The bicycle lane is to the right, vehicular traffic to the far right. There is no need for car parks in Xinxiang, but bicycle parking areas are everywhere. The parking fee is usually about two cents, payable to "minders" (usually older women) who guard the bikes against theft.

A residential area on the north bank of Xinxiang's Wei River whose waters eventually flow into the Gulf of Chihli. The river is out of view to the right—below the high flood wall seen here. The sign says: "Those who want cement, sand, tiles or gravel, please go to the east."

Looking across to the south bank of the Wei River. The river is out of view just below the trees and flood wall in the foreground.

A docile calf being led to the slaughter.

A pair of porkers on their way to market down Jianshe Road. The ill-natured peasant driving them is momentarily "out of the picture," waving his stick at me. For some reason, he objected to his beasts being photographed.

Pepper, whole or ground, on sale in land-locked Xinxiang's incomprehensibly-named "Eastern Sea Market."

A vegetable stand on Jianshe Road.

Privacy is at a premium in teeming China's choked cities, and parks provide one of the few "getaways" for courting couples. This romantic scene awaits young lovers in Xinxiang's "People's Park."

Jianshe Road in autumn.

Three stores on Jianshe Road. The store to the left is a restaurant featuring roast chicken and rabbit meat. In the middle is an electrical appliance repair shop. The store to the right has nets, lines and other fishing equipment useful at the artificial fishing ponds which surround Xinxiang.

China's coal-fired economy brings another smoggy day to Xinxiang.

Bird sellers on Victory Bridge.

A basket seller on a city lane.

Another humble Xinxiang home whose owner appreciates beauty.

Dining on the cheap at one of Xinxiang's hundreds of out-door, squat-stool eateries.

A convenience store. Though most Chinese are atheists, they are simultaneously highly superstitious. Virtually every private portal in China bears red "Good Fortune" strips on jambs and lintels. The strips are annually renewed at the commencement of the lunar new year.

When your bike breaks down in Xinxiang, you are rarely more than a block or two from a curbside repair shop. Here Yang Lian Zsi, a 43-year-old woman mechanic, makes running repairs.

"The first thing you will notice upon entering Henan Normal University is a 20-foot-tall granite Mao standing atop a pedestal. He stands serene and smug, with a hint of a smile, possibly unaware of his waning popularity in the more modern, cynical metropolises of coastal China."

The main gate to Henan Normal University with Number One Building (which houses the English Department) in the background. The red-on-white banner in the foreground advertises pan bread with fried egg stuffing for sale.

Henan Normal University's faculty and staff members, who, along with their families, number 10,000, are housed on campus in 43 apartment blocks like these shown above and below.

The University's auditorium. The brass characters across the entryways proclaim: "Teaching is the most glorious profession in the world."

Acceptance into Henan Normal University's Fine Arts Department is partly based on performance testing of candidates' artistic skills. Here some high school seniors, prospective music teachers, arrive for a week of auditioning. The gold-on-red banner announces: "The Musical Department welcomes you."

The University's 10,000 resident students live in just nine dormitory buildings like this one: West Dormitory Number Five—a girls' dormitory. "The students are packed in— packed in tight. They live in dormitory rooms 16 feet long by 10 feet wide (160 square feet), eight students to a room. That works out to 20 square feet per person. Imagine it! Mark off a square four-and-a-half feet by four-and-a-half feet on the floor. Now stand inside it. Okay, that's your share of the room." The rooms are heatless and with floors of bare concrete.

A concrete ping-pong table outside the boys' Middle Dormitory Number Two.

The University's coal-fired steam plant complex.

Mandatory military training for both males and females is a prerequisite for acquiring a university degree in China. Here students stand at attention before their trainers. The white-on-red banner proclaims: "Teaching, educating, facing the New Century. Cultivating more creative and competent intellectuals."

The farming village of Bai Fu Mang in the foothills of the Taihang Shan in northern Henan.

Mr. Wang Fusuo, Zoe's uncle, standing in front of his home in Bai Fu Mang.

The home's courtyard. Notice the red "dui lian" (good luck strips) above and beside each portal opening off the courtyard.

The terraced fields surrounding Bai Fu Mang. The yellow field in the foreground is mustard in bloom. The fields in the background are winter wheat.

Zoe (Wang Yun), the only university graduate the village of Bai Fu Mang has ever produced, standing before her father's wheat field. The primary school she attended is in the background.

The friendly faces of China. The author being mobbed by school children in a public park.

Young Chinese Voices

Westerners frequently and fairly criticize the Chinese government's harsh management of their society. It is impossible to overlook the regime's authoritarianism, its disregard of democratic principles, its refusal to protect basic human rights. And yet, if one actually lives within the society, one would almost have to conclude that the oppression sits very lightly on most Chinese shoulders. College students, for instance, remain intensely patriotic and are optimistic of both their personal prospects and their nation's prospects. The disaffected student radicals of Beijing University who led the 1989 Tiananmen Square demonstrations would hardly seem representative of the nation's college youth as a whole. Most of the young people seem to be fully supportive of post-Mao government.

And, it must be said, China *is* doing something right in the manner in which it is raising its children. Chinese youth, almost invariably products of intact families, do not display anywhere near the degree of alienation, cynicism and pessimism common amongst their college counterparts in Europe or America. Chinese students are not bored, are not sarcastic, are not disrespectful, and are not contemptuous of their society or their elders. In short, Chinese youth are not spoiled.

117

I would challenge anyone to find a Western college with students who could produce sample introductory essays as heartening and wholesome as these written by my English Composition students at Henan Normal University.

Class One: English Writing

Ren Sifei—"Grass"

Do you want to know me? Maybe you can get some interesting things from me. Now, I want to introduce me to you briefly.

My Chinese name is Ren Sifei, meaning I want to fly like a bird in wide sky. My farmer parents give me birth in 1979. My hometown is a mountain area, that is, a beautiful place. Which brings up me knowledge and ability. With time flying, I have been realizing that my hometown is more backward than other places. That makes me sad. At the same time I make up my mind to change those bad things.

With a great wish I entered Henan Normal University in 1998. I deeply know knowledge is strength. My hometown in bad need of many teachers. I want to be a good teacher for my hometown.

In order to became a good teacher, I do a lot of things to improve my ability. One of them is studying more my majors. My majors are not easy for me and there is a long way before me to go. At the other way, I choose some notions to develop my other abilities, I try to learn computer.

I have a lot of hobbies. I like listening music, dancing and playing table tennis. Reading is a most big hobby. I'm also humorous, I think. I'm quite talkative. To tell you the truth, the most happy thing for me is chatting with others. Oh, travelling is also good.

Wang Sumei—"Lucie"

Dear Sir. I am very glad to introduce myself to you.
I was born in a small town near the Yellow River in 1978. I have a very happy family. So kind mother, father and naughty little brother. Being delicately brought up, mother took care of me very tenderly. Now I grew into a healthy and lovely girl.
My temperament is like inside, perhaps a little outside. I like singing, drawing. I'd also like to listen classic Chinese and English songs and music. But I think it is

my most favourite thing to read a good book. I love reading books very much. Before university I had many famous literary books in China and classic European and American articles, stories and books in Chinese. I like many famous writers. Such as: Shakespeare, Dickens, Mark Twain, O'Henry and so on. I felt their books is pretty excellent. I think English is very helpful and useful for me to learn more foreign literatures and knowledge. I felt English is beautiful as same as Chinese. Now I entered the university. I have more chance, more time to learn English and read English books, in English Department. I believe I will try my best to learn more things.

Dear Mr. Adams, I love Lucie and her temperament, her experience, her lovely in "A Tale of Two Cities" by Dickens. So I named Lucie. Mr. Adams, I also want to say, as your student, I'm so glad. I'm really happy. I hope you get along well with us. Thank you!

Zhang Xiao Xiang—"Edward"

My name is Zhang Xiao Xiang. This is my Chinese name, and my English name is Edward. I come from a remote village. There are few students who can enter University. I'm also the only one in my family of history. So I feel very fortunate. My parents and my relations are very glad when I enter Henan Normal University.

When I was in my childhood, there was a student who passed the entrance to University in my village. Then my parents encouraged me to learn from him. I haven't realized what's University. But I could guess University must be a good place from my parents' eyes. Then he becomes my example. When I went to the primary school, I study very hard and my teachers like me very much. Naturally I enter University.

Before entering University, I'm a quiet boy. I have nothing to do except study. But when I enter University, I become active and talkative. I think it is very necessary for me. I like sports. For example, I like an active part in sports meet. Coming a remote and strange city, I should depend on myself. Now I'm growing up I must learn to stand on my own two feet. I think nothing is difficult if I put my heart into it. I believe I can do well with everything.

I like teacher. Teacher is the most glorious profession in the world. So I enter Henan Normal University. I decide to make our country stronger and stronger with my knowledge.

Shao Yanhui—"Jan"

I am glad to introduce myself to you. Being born in a happy family I have sister and brother and they are all much older than me. My brother has two daughters and my sister has a son and a daughter. I love their children very much. It is incredible that I have grown from a tomboy into a graceful girl! The joys of childhood are most impressive. Though I am 20 years old now, sometimes my behavior is not particularly adult. In my parents' eyes, I am always a little girl.

The period of Primary School, I tried my best to be a good student. In Secondary School, my attention always relaxs and my lessons were not very good. Eventually I lost the chance of entered an Emphatic Advanced School. I was depressed about this. I should have encouraged myself to grasp the opportunity. I should have warned myself that time lost can not be won again. I should have . . . But I was not. So now I have to stay here, as a informal student. The memories are painful and disheartening. I had lost many thing. I must try to work hard for the present and to won a splendid future, for my families and myself. My parents are almost sixty and my father is busy with the business throughout the year. I know they hope I could have a good job.

Well, I like to dream. I want to be a wanderer and I can spend all my life wandering the world. As a matter of fact, my dream can not come true forever. I am eager to read books. Then I can know much Chinese culture and European culture, American culture, and so on. My brother bought many books for me when I was a little girl. I am very grateful for him. I am also interested in music and I love to sing, though I often sing in tune. The most awful thing is my handwriting. I'll try to improve it. From the introduction, do you remember me?

He Xiaocun—"Lily"

I'm a Chinese girl. My name is He Xiaocun. Now I have an English name, it's Lily. I come from Zhengzhou—the capital of Henan Province.

There are five people in my family: father, mother, brother, sister and I. My father is a worker. He puts his heart into his work and now he has been an engineer. My mother is a present. She is very kind. My brother is a worker, too. He was married two years ago, and I am coming to be an aunt. Sister is an English teacher. We get on well with each other. In my family I feel very happy and lucky.

I have been interested in English when I was studying at primary school. At that time my sister was a Middle-School student. She often read English when she went back home every day. I showed great interest on it, so she began to teach me how to speak and write English words. It was the beginning of my English studying. During the Middle-School I like to study English very much, and I always won the first in my class. When I graduated from high-school, I chose the English Department of Henan Normal University. I was lucky that I have been studying here for one year.

China is a great country with long history, but she is still backward. Now English is a very useful language in the world. Someone has foresaid that: English would be one of the passcards people went into 21 century with. I think it quite true. So I must study it carefully and work hard for my country.

I am talkative. I like to talk with every people around me. In my spare time I like playing table-tennis. I like sports games showed on TV. I think healthy is very important to everyone.

At last I hope I can make more friends in the future.

Class Two: English Writing

Gu Ying—"Rosalind"

I'm Rosalind. I'm 18 years old. I was born in Shanghai, but I have been living in Xinxiang. All of my dear relations are in Shanghai, so I'm willing to go back to my hometown. My father is an engineer and my mum is a doctor. They love me, their only child, very much. But at the same time, they are strict with me. You know, in China, parents always put the hopes on their children.

I always wished that I can have a brother or sister in childhood, because I felt alone and I needed friends. Mum knew me well, so she taught me to love music. From the music, I knew how to get the happiness by myself. But also I knew how to control myself. Maybe for this reason, I always can face the life pleasantly.

I think I'm a person who is willing to receive new things. I hate the old, dischangable things. But for the good, old traditional things, I always keep them. I always get well with others and not only in spare time but also in work and study. I like to change my minds with my friends. From others' minds, I can get many useful things. So, I'd like to make friends with you. If that, I can get many knowledge in America. Thank you!

Han Hong Yan—"Hank"

I am Hank with the Chinese name: Han Hong Yan. I was born in 28 September, 1978. I grew up in countryside. I came from a poor family in a remote town. My parents are both farmers but in fact they have little experience in farming, so we are always short of money. Thus my father warn me to study harder and obtain more knowledge. I have a young sister and a brother who are reading in the middle school.

As a student of English, I don't do well in English. Because at middle school we're always studying grammar. Being backward, it's impossible for us to practice English speaking and listening. After entering this university, I have more time to practice my oral

English but I still have a long way to go. I hope I can improve me with the help of Dr. Adams.

Besides English, I still love music. But I can't play a single musical instrument. I only love appreciating songs and singing them in my own way. I am inward in character so I am not much of a talker, in fact I like to be silent. Someway I am diffident.

As a method of practising English, I'll insist on writing journal. I'd like to share my teacher's joy and make our work better.

Li Wang—"Hilton"

My name is Hilton, 20 years old.

I'm from a worker's family, not very rich but very pleasant. My father lost his work two years ago, but he bought a car to do some business. Though he's very busy in business, he calls me every weeked to say he loves me. My mother is out of work for many years, she do many work in house. They love each other. Peipei is my young sister, a very beautiful girl. She is so confident that she always asks me: "Is me the best beauty in the world?" What a naughty girl. My parents love my sister and I very much, of course we all love them.

I like to learning English very much, because I began listening VOA (Voice of America) two years ago. Now my listening ability is improved notably. But I'm poor in speaking English. My spoken English is my big headache of the year. I'll do my best in the future.

In my spare time, I listens the music or the songs. In the weekend, I always play the basketball or table tennis with my roommate.

This is the first time that a foreign teacher teach me. I'm very excited. I decided: I'll speak the English like a native speaker: idiomatic and fluent. Though that is very difficult, I'll do my best.

Wang Zhiping—"Fish"

I am Wang Zhiping. It's my
Chinese name. My English name is
FISH. I'm not very tall, so I always
want to grow fast and fast. Then I can
do everything such as playing basketball and football, running fast. All the
same I can take the first place in the
sports events. I'm longing for this day.

I am an ordinary-looking boy: so
everything seems not to be smooth.
Sometimes I felt depressed and sad,
but I didn't lose my confidence. I believe I can do something very useful
for other people. In order to make up for my fault, I'm devoted to
learning everything well. Step by step. I find I am able to do something successful. Which gives me more confidence. After a long
hard work, I made great progress. I passed the examination to the
entrance of university. Finally I came to the Henan Teacher Normal
University. My heart was more strong that where there is a will
there is a way.

In the university I must study hard and make progress everyday and improve my general English levels.

I'll be an excellent teacher in the future. I can do it successfully. I believe it.

Li Juan—"Wendy"

I'm Wendy. I'm in Grade Two this year. Looking back, I was
born in 1980. In my family, I have parents, my grandparents and my
little brother. Of course, I love them very much.

I come from Zhengzhou. And I'm glad to serve it after graduation. My hometown is still not too rich. I'll do my best to work,
to teach my students in the future.

It's difficult to say which type my character lies in. Sometimes
I like playing and talking with others, but sometimes I feel it's bad
to do that. Maybe it's all because I'm a younger. Everything seems

interesting to me. And it makes my tem-
per changeable.

Now, I major in English. It's very
useful in our society. But I feel I have to
try my best to improve my oral English
and listening. It's hard, but I know I must
do well.

In my spare time, I like talking with
my friends, like reading periodical. And
I'm a filmfan. I like children. They always
let me happy. I like all kinds of festival.
On these days, all the people enjoy themselves.

I like listening songs, too. But to my sadness, I feel I'm fat,
and it often makes me diffident. But I can get rid of this idea by myself, I think.

Class Three: English Writing

Liu Yonghua—"Susan"

My name is Susan, and my
Chinese name is Liu Yonghua. I come
from a lovely city, Hebi, which in the
north of Henan Province.

I went to college in 1998 and
now I have been a second-year student. Last month, we were given an
Army Training. It was tiring but very
interesting. During the time, we were
in high spirits. We know we were
training for protecting our dear
country once we were needed some
day. The National Day is coming, all
the Chinese people are excited. The People's Republic of China, our
lovely mother, will spend her fiftieth birthday and undoubtly, we regard it as a proud. The traditional festival, semi-Autumn, is coming
too. On that night all the Chinese families surround the tables, appreciating the bright moon. If one of their natives isn't at home, the

others will be missing him very much. On the other hand, the man out always raises his head to the moon, missing his home town and his families. On this day, there are many kinds of delicious food, such as fresh fruits and cakes, especially the moon cakes.

Oh, now I can't help missing my parents, my elder brother and my young sister! How I miss them! Dear moon, please take my regards to my families and my friends, will you?

I'm sorry, I forget the meaning of the word, Autobiography, I made a mistake, didn't I?

Li Jun-de—"Dean"

My Chinese name is Li Jun-de, and I was born in a countryside. Then I went to school and studied in my hometown, until last year I entered this university.

In my hometown, there are many fields and mountain. I like them, though they are common. I think that they come into being a beautiful scene. To a large plain, I don't like it too much, I would tell there is a lack of something.

I appreciate and enjoy all the beautiful things, such as comfortable essay, some art works, some quiet and beautiful scenes of nature for they can relax me and make me happy. When I stand in this surrounding, I would forget my trouble, unpleasant things and the time. And I like drawing and listening the slower music and so on.

In my studies, my English is common or poor. Vocabulary speaking and listening are not well. I haven't lost too much time, but I'm still such. In this term, I'll study harder than before, and I'll improve my studying method, to catch up with my classmates.

I enjoy simple, so I often have not many words to speak with other people. Sometime I feel lonely, but sometime it can give me a quiet and free time and space, let me think about many things.

Wang Ling—"Violin"

I came to this world on August 20, 1980. Generally, the children are named by their grandparents, so I had a name Wang Lijuan after being born. After I attended junior school, my father gave me a formal name, that is, Wang Ling. When I entered University, an English name was needed, so I chose a word which has similar pronunciation with my Chinese name as my new name. It is Violin.

My father is a teacher. He has been teaching for 23 years. He was engaged in this profession since he was 19 years old. My mother is in charge of the housework. She is a good assistant of my father. I like my parents.

I have two sisters and one brother. They are all younger than me. It is a little unbelievable now, but that's true. Many Chinese like boys. They wouldn't give up until they had one. To change the view is a bit difficult, especially in the country. But now, with the development of society, it has been greatly changed.

I like to do many things, because I am changeable. I like playing table tennis and basketball. This term I choose basketball as my major P.E. course.

The important task of me is to do well in my courses and to make friends.

That's all. Thank you giving me a chance to express myself.

Good wishes to you.

Song Peiru—"Sandy"

My name is Sandy. Why do I call myself Sandy? Because Sandy's pronunciation is the same as Sunday's. I like Sunday most of a week. I call myself Sandy. The second cause is that it means sun-shining. In my life, the happy things are more than sad things.

I like smiling. My friends always tell me that my smile is just like sun-shining.

I come from LuoYang. LuoYang is a very beautiful city. There is a long history behind her. There are a lot of famous scenic spots in LuoYang. Every scenic spot has its own story. For example, Long Mei has a lot of moving stories. LuoYang is famous because not only her scenic spots but also her flower named MuDan. MuDan is the king of the flowers. She is so beautiful that so many people who come from diffentent places go to appreciate her. Every year, when April is coming, each street of LuoYang is dotted by this lovely flowers. How wonderful!

There are four person in my family. My father and my sister both are teachers. But my father teach Chinese. My sister teach Physics. They work in different middle school. My mother is a worker. They all work hard. I love them, they love me, too.

My family is a happy family. My parents are my friends. When I meet difficulties, I will tell them. They try their best to help me. I learn a lot of good things from them.

I love them, I love my family.

Cheng Yaoping—"Pindar"

I'm a common girl, and come from a peasant family. I love everyone in my family: grandmother, parents, two younger sisters. Sure, they love me very much. My grandmother is eighty-four years, very old, but she is still in good health. She often tells me some ideas of living cause my parents are industrious peasants. They work hard to supply my family, especially my father, he is very strict, mild. He always asks us to help others. He also said to me: Struggle and plain living. I'm obliged of him. Two younger sisters are very beautiful and clever, they often bring laugh to my family.

I'm a failure in my study. After I finished study in senior

school, I went back home, then worked in middle school. A year later, I realized my knowledge is limited; so I decided to go to school. But I felt difficult to study hard, because I wanted to play. Another year past, I didn't get anything. I'm sorry for that. New Term began. I wished I could be strict with me, and improved my English study.

I'm shy, and I'm not good at talking. I'm afraid to answer questions. I have many hobbies: writing, reading, travel, ride horse, e.g. when I get a good novel, I must finish reading in a time.

Though I'm a shy girl, I'm very enthusim. I like everything good. Today, I have renew myself. I must get rid of my bad habit and to work harder.

At Last, welcome you to China and "Merry Middle Autumn Festival to You and Your Friends." Wish you like here!

Class Four: English Writing

Hu Hai-zhu—"Rosalind"

My name is Hu Hai-zhu. I'm from Luohe, Henan. I have a very warm family. Both my parents are farmers. They work hard on the farm. I have two brothers and I am the youngest of us three. Both my brothers have been married. They lead a happy life. They have three children all together. They are all naughty, but I still love them.

What makes me different from others is that I like laughing. And, I never walk a step and a step. If you see a little (I am short) girl in the street who walk jumping and laughing like a bird, that's me.

Qin Qing Ling—"Lorna"

My Chinese name is QIN QING LING. Yesterday when we had Oral English course I had not prepared my English name. So when our teacher asked me for my English name, I had to go through my dictionary to look for one. At last I decided to use 'LORNA' as my English name. But I don't know what it mean still.

Now I'd like to introduce myself to you.

I was born on June 1, 1979. My hometown is a big town in AnYang 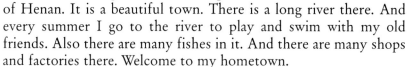 of Henan. It is a beautiful town. There is a long river there. And every summer I go to the river to play and swim with my old friends. Also there are many fishes in it. And there are many shops and factories there. Welcome to my hometown.

My father is a worker, and my mother is a farmer. They are both warm-hearted and kind. I have two brothers. My elder brother has been married and I have a niece about two years old now. My sister-in-law is very beautiful and she shows filial obedience. My second brother is a worker, too. I always treat him as one of my friends. If I am unhappy, I often refer to him. My family is very cozy. I love it very much.

I like singing. I often listen to music and then learn it. If I have a chance, I will sing to you. And I like reading story-books and watching TV. That's why my eyesight is so poor.

I like English very much. My brothers like English, too. So before I began to learn English, they had taught me it for about one year. I enjoyed myself in it. But my speaking and listening are not good, even bad. I am very worried. I am afraid when I graduate I am not fit for my job. So I decided to try my best to work harder, to learn English, especially listening, speaking, reading, writing and translating. I trust I'll success. Because my dream is to be a teacher. If I want to be a teacher I must do that.

Thank you.

Jian Zhen Ying—"Jane"

I'm Jane. This is my English name. My Chinese name is Jian Zhen Ying. Now, I'm studying in the Foreign Language Department of Henan Normal University. I'm in Class 4. Grade 2.

My hometown is in the south of Henan Province. That's a small town, not very rich, but very beautiful. My hometown has a long history, the famous ancient general Fanli was born there.

There are five people in my family. My father, mother, two brothers and I. My father is a teacher. He teaches Chinese in a primary school. My father loves his students, he always works hard. My mother is a traditional Chinese woman, I think. Every day she is busy, though she hasn't a job. She is busy doing cooking, washing, sewing, and so on. My mother often says such a sentence: housework is such a thing that you will never finish it. But mother never complain anything. My two brothers are both pupils. As other little boys, they are naughty sometimes. But both of them study well. In my family, parents love three children, and three children love and respect parents. So, you know, I have a happy family.

Now, it's the time to introduce myself. I'm nineteen this year. My 19th birthday will be celebrated on the first day of 2000. That's wonderful. But I can't go home to stay with my families on that day, that's a pity! When I miss my families, I like going to see a film. I also like reading novels, and listening to popular songs.

The most different point in my characters, with other girls, is that I like smiling. I will smile when I am happy, and when I am unhappy, I will smile too. Because I believe such a sentence: Smile can keep person young forever.

Zhao Jingli—"Zoe"

My Chinese name is Zhao Jingli. And I also have an English name Zoe. I'm nineteen years old now. I come from LuoYang. It isn't a large city, but it is an old city. It has a long history. It has ever been capitals of six dynasty.

I have a large family. There are six people in my family. My father, my mother, my grandmother, two brothers and I. Because I'm not the only daughter in my family, I must share my parents' love with my brothers. I can do a lot of things at home. I usually help my mother do some odds and ends. I'm a docile daughter in my family. My parents love me very much and I love them.

I have two hobbies. One is enjoying music, especially Chinese folk music and pop music, but I can't stand modern jazz. The other is reading novels, especially works of Qiong Yao. Qiong Yao's books are very popular in my country. Most of them tell us romantic love stories. Some people think that reading romantic novels is complete waste of time, but I don't think so.

My ideal profession is teacher. Perhaps three years later I will realize my dream. In order to become a capable and competent English teacher, I must study hard now.

I don't have some unique characters. I'm a common girl. I like things that most people like and I hate things that most people hate. If I have a unique character, that is perseverence. Because I know an English saying "Perseverence overcomes all things."

Zhang Haiyan—"Kate"

My name is Kate, which is my English name. I didn't have it until I had a foreign teacher. My Chinese name is Zhang Haiyan. I was born in a small village of Henan Province in 1981. I am the youngest girl of my family, and for this reason, my parents pay great

attention to my education. I went to
the primary school at the age of 5
while other children of my village were
playing around. Moreover, I could
continue my education after graduation from Secondary School while
many children had to quit school.

I am fond of languages, both
Chinese and English, although I don't
have a gift for languages. When I
began to learn English, I always failed
the exam. But I believed "no pains, no
gains." I was sure I could get high
grades through hard work. That's also
why I can stay here in the university.

I used to keep a journal, but somehow I gave it up. I've always
been an impatient girl. I'm fed up of doing the same thing everyday.
But since you require us to keep a journal, Sir, I'll do it as you say.
And I'm sure I can do it well. There is an old saying: "Constant
dripping wears stone." I'll always keep it in mind. I hope I can do
well in my writing course.

Class Five: English Writing

Qin Xiang—"Martha"

My name is Qin Xiang, MARTHA is my first English name.
I'm twenty years old. Yes. I'm older than most of us. I come from
a farmer's family. As we know, the education in countryside is poor
in China. I have felt it since I entered this university. My knowledge
is more limited than some students. Oral English is not good, and
listening power is poor, for most times I can't understand you. I
often take a loss.

Knowing my shortcomings, I see I must try my best to catch
up with my classmates.

I admire my parents. Mother has died for her four children. I
often see her in dreams. Father is still working in the fields. I love
him very much. No him. No me. I have three elder brothers, two of

whom have married. My second brother is working in Xinxiang. So I don't feel lonely.

I like English very much and like watching foreign films. (The stories are excellent.) And I'm fond of listening English songs. (They are full of general motion). Quiet life fits me and I'm keen on sports. Sports keep me healthy and slim. Playing PingPong is my favorite game at present. I think when I touch a new game, I will like it too.

I'm happy to make friends any-where and anytime. I hope they are honest and not liars. If they are not, I will cut the touch with them.

My home town is Boai, Jiaozhuo. Jiaozhuo is a beautiful city. She has some very good scenes to travel. Invite you and your fam-ily to our city from my bottom of heart.

Zuo Wei—"Wendy"

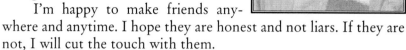

Nice to meet you. It's my hon-our to be your student. My Chinese name is Zuo Wei. I'm going ninteen. I'm a native of Xinxiang. My father is a Chinese teacher. He works in the NO.2 middle school. My mother is a nurse. I'm the only child of my fam-ily. I think my family is a happy one. It's only ten minutes walk from here to my family, so I live at home. If you are free, welcome to my family.

Xinxiang is not a big city but a lovely city. She is changing and de-veloping. I hope you can lead a happy life here.

I like reading novels. The novel that I like best is Gone With The Wind. I like not only reading but also travelling. I have been to Beijing, the capital of China, TianJing, Da Lian and so on. This summer, I went to Beijing. She is a city with long history. Someone is interested in the history of Beijing. But I think today's Beijing is more beautiful. Now, she is still Chinese center of culture, economy.

I like my motherland, but I also like USA. I learned something about her from book, TV and film. She is the most developed country in the world. In many respect, she is advanced. If I have chance, I hope I can go to USA to study further.

At last, welcome you to China. I hope you have a good time in Xinxiang, in China.

Zhao Dong Ya—"Helen"

I am sure you can call me Helen. My Chinese name is Zhao Dong Ya. I come from a small city and it may be one third of Xinxiang. Although it's very small, it developed very quickly recent years. And I think it's beautiful.

I've already nineteen. Fortunately I can pass the examination and come to this university. When I was a high school student, I worked very hard. Everyday I only study and study, so I have no time to play and I have no interesting things. I don't like sports, when I have P.E. class, I'll have a headache.

I think it's a enjoy that read books in bed. And if there was something to eat or drink, that's better. I hate to be disturbed when I am paying attention to a novel. Maybe I'll shout at him. I'm short of sight because I usually read books in bed. I think it's a regret.

I like travelling by myself. But there is only one child in my family and it's me. So my parents don't let me go myself. I think I can't have a good time with my parents. So I seldom travel by now. Since I came here, I realise that it's a happy thing I can do many things with my parents. But it's late. There were six hundred kilometers between two cities. I can't go home easy. I'm very sorry about it and if I have chance I'll apologize to my parents.

Because of some reasons, I have few friends. I ever want to make many friends and I try my best. But the result is disappointing. I like sitting on lawn and seeing the sky, the cloud and the birds without any words. But almost nobody has the same favor, so I have to do it alone.

As a foreign language department student, I want to know more thing about foreign country. I want to know how they live and work, how they spend their spare time, how they receive the education, how they deal with some questions of their families. And I want to taste the food of most countries. Maybe it's funny but it's true and I'll try to know the fact.

Yuan Qiu Li—"Rebecca"

My Chinese name is Yuan Qiu Li. I'm from Zhu Ma Dian city. It is famous as neither a beautiful place nor a rich city, but it is famous as the poorest city in China. Though my hometown is very poor, I love it very much, because it brought me up and gave me a lot.

I'm the first child of my parents. I have one young sister and one young brother. I like them and they like me too. My parents are both peasant, they work hard to support our family. I love and repect my parents. My family is not rich, but is very happy.

I'm a shy girl and not a much talker, especially when I face many people. I always feel nervous. Sometimes I think I must change myself. So I try to speak more when there are many people, the result is not very good, but I have made some progress. I decided to go on and do my best to change myself. I believe I'll become not a shy girl in the future.

I hate sports and pay no attention to it, so last term I failed it. I had to be examed for it. In my free time, I like reading books especially foreign books. I read some foreign novels in English, but I couldn't understand all them. I decided to continue read them to improve my English.

Guo Junfang—"Rosanna"

My name is Guo Junfang, English name is ROSANNA. 20 years old. I'm from Lin Zhou, Henan province.

In my family, I have my mother, father, brother and sister-in-law. I entered Henan Normal University in 1998. I major in English Education. I like to be an English teacher. I like our school.

I like sports, music, especially drawing. Since I entered the university, I have being drawing for our Foreign Language Department. I feel very happy for what I did.

China is a developing country, which is a little backward. The condition of our school is not very good. So we feel lucky, because we have two foreign teachers. Chinese Education System is not very reasonable, most students can't speak English freely. I hope we can make rapid progress under your help. I also hope we'll become true friends in future days.

It's my first time to talk to a foreigner just like I did today. I feel excited, but I also found out I have a long way to walk during I study English. I can't understand you easily at class. I hope you'll teacher us patiently.

Thank you!

Your true friend
ROSANNA

Class Six: English Writing for Tourism Students

Zhao Dujuan—"Jenny"

I'm glad to meet you! My Chinese name is ZHAO DUJUAN. My English name is JENNY. I like my English name very much. I'm nineteen. I was born in SanMenxia, so SanMenxia is my hometown. She is a small and beautiful city of tourism. SanMenxia lies in the west of Henan. The traffic is very convenient, and the products are very plentiful. My hometown also is an industrial city. The main products are gold and coal. Besides, "SanMenXia Apples" are very famous in China. There are some tourism natural resources, for example, Hot Spring, the Yellow River visit place, YaWu mountain, Han Gu fort, and so on. "The Yello River Travel Holiday" is hold once of three years. I love my hometown. Welcome to SanMenxia.

I have a happy family which is made up of father, mother and I. My father is a government official. He is a humorous man. He likes to make fun of other people. His interest is to go fishing. I love my father. My mother is an excellent accountant. She likes to play the table tennis. She also likes singing and dancing. I love my mother.

I am the only child in my family, so my parents are all love me, but they are strict with my study. They wish that I could become a useful people. I will study hard. I like dancing and singing. Although I have no a good voice, I still love singing. I also like music very much.

I wish that I can get well with you. I want to learn a lot of knowledge with you.

I'm glad to meet you!

Li Dan—"Linda"

Dr. William Adams, "Gold to see you."
My name is Li Dan. My English name is Linda. Thank you give me an English name. I come from An Yang. An Yang is an old city and a historic city. Do you know Jia Gu Wen? They have been discovered in my home town. If you free, I hope you and your family come to my home town.

In fact, my English is poor, because I have never gone to high school. I had learned tourism for three years. So I come from tourism school. I like tour, I want to go everywhere. English is important to me. So I must study English. If I can do it, I can talk with you even everyone, and go out to see the world.

In my free time, I often go shopping and eat something. So I'm a fat girl. I want lose pound, but I can't get it. Do you know any good ideas? If you know, please tell me, of course, I often read some novels. For example, "Jane Eyre," "Wuthering" etc.

At last, I hope you speak slowly in the class and I hope you can help me. Thank you very much.

That's all!

Chen Yingjie—"Sharon"

Welcome you to China to be a college teacher. I'm very glad to meet you. When I heard we would have a foreign teacher to teach us, I felt very excited. But after this class, I feel better than before. I think I'll improve my English with your help.

My Chinese name is CHEN YINGJIE. I haven't brothers or sisters. But my parents love me very much and I love them also. My hometown is Luo Yang. Did you hear she? She is the second biggest city in Henan. Have you ever been there? She is a beautiful city. A lot of people went to there to see "MuDan flower" (sorry, I don't know how to spell MuDan in English), because there is a sentence: "Luo Yang MuDan flower is the best in the world."

I like English very much. When I was young, I thought I'll be a tour-guide. English is a world language. If someone want to be a tour-guide, he or she must to be learn English. These years lots of foreign people come to China, as a college student, I must study English. Except English I like to read some books. I think book can give me a lot of knowledge. As the other girls, I also like dancing and singing, but I can't do that very well.

I'm very glad you can teach us. I think you can improve our English, you must think so, mustn't you?

Yang Ping—"Ellen"

I'm very glad to meet you! My name is Yang Ping. English name is Ellen. I'm eighteen years old. I come from Xu Chang. My home-town is a beautiful city, but it is not very large. She has a lot of beautiful place. Such as temple of Guan Yu, brige of Ba Ling, or another place. Welcome to visit my city: (hometown).

I'm second year student. Henan Normal University is a big school. I'd like to study in this school. I'd like to sing a song, play or read another book. My English is poor. I feel very silly. I decided to study English very hard, but the effect is not good. I hope you can help me to learn English. I think in the future days, we can get well with you. We can made a good friend. My age isn't old. So I often miss my father and my mother. They are business. So they are very busy. I often called to them. My family is very warm!

After look at your photos, I feel you have a happy family. At the end of I want to say: You are my first foreign teacher. I feel very lucky to meet you!

Hu Liuxi—"Crystal"

My Chinese name is Hu Liuxi. I come from Zhu Madian. I'm glad to meet you here. Now let me introduce myself. Thank you for giving me an English name. I like it very much.

I graduated from MAXING MIDDLE SCHOOL. I was born in RUNAN. My parents are peasant. Four years ago my mother died. I have one older sister and younger brother. My hometown is very beautiful. Because it is a countryside, air is clear. There is a lake named SU YA LAKE near to my hometown. Every summer vacation I can go swimming in it and every winter vacation I can go skating on it. When I was not happy I often go there. I can go boating whenever I would like to.

When I was young I went to there with my partners. That day, wind was very strong. It's very cold. We were going to go boating because this was my first going boating. We were very nervous. Unfortunately, we dropped into the lake. Help. Help! we shouted and cried. A stranger saved us. We grated him very much. But I like it very much. I missed my childhood there.

Town of my hometown is very small but if you go there you can visit many many places. Such as: MANHAICHANSHI. It is said that it is the biggest Chanshi in China. Though my hometown tourism is not too developed.

As my English writing is limited, I can't describe my hometown correctly. I know it is a good place to visit. Welcome to my hometown.

Welcome, Welcome!

A Trip to Beijing

In September all of my students—male and female—were re-
moved from class for mandatory military training. They were issued
rifles and PLA khaki-green uniforms with scarlet shoulder boards.
Then they learned to march. At first they were comically inept: always out of step as they trooped up and down the campus streets,
and whenever a halt was called rear ranks would unfailingly accor-
dion up into front ranks while the frustrated instructors, PLA reg-
ulars, raced about screaming. But these student-soldiers quickly got
better. The Chinese seemingly take to regimentation as naturally
and enthusiastically as Germans, and soon these students of mine,
especially the female squads, were a scary sight. They'd march along
in perfect lock-step with red flags and banners borne aloft, bellowing out the cadence in their piercing voices. It seemed a good time
to get out of town for awhile, so Roselyn and I decided to go up to
Beijing for a week.

We boarded a northbound train on a platform at Xinxiang. At
the next platform over a southbound passenger train sat idling. This
train looked the way a train should look. Passenger cars in flat
hunter green livery with yellow pinstripes. Inbound from Mongolia,
it had crossed the Gobi and looked like it. Hard travelled. Diesel
stains on the locomotive, dust plumes caked onto the car skirtings.

Our train, on the other hand, did not look the way a train should look. Nothing romantic about it. Disgustingly modern with one of those aerodynamic, wedge-faced electric locomotives with the thin edge of the wedge sitting just above the tracks. Double-decker passenger cars in gay silver and blue livery.

Chinese trains are perfectly punctual, and we are barely seated before the train starts to surge to its 120 kph running speed. Smooth cushion ride on seamless tracks.

Chinese trains have five "grades" of accommodation. These are *not* referred to as "classes," designations which would be gauche in this ostensibly classless society. Still, the "grades" tell their own story. The grades are "soft sleep," "hard sleep," "soft sit," "hard sit" and "hard stand."

Our particular grade is "soft sit," accommodation for which I've paid U.S. $11 per ticket for the 400-mile trip. For this price we get nicely cushioned seats, armrest doilies, frilly curtains. We sit in a non-compartmentalized car not unlike economy airline seating but more convivial since every other row of seats is turned around so six people sit facing each other across a tiny table, while across the center aisle four people sit facing one another. The passengers here are mostly from what passes as middle-class and lower-middle class in China—people that might even own motor scooters rather than bikes (but certainly not cars), people that might possess five or more sets of clothing—small businessmen, mid-level bureau-crats, high school and college teachers, poorly-paid doctors. The luggage in the racks—a good indicator of this particular car's col-lective wealth—ranges from decent vinyl suitcases, to clear plastic zip-up cases saved from bed-clothing purchases which reveal the owners' travel gear (shirts, shoes, bras, underwear, gifts, food sup-plies), to taped-up cardboard boxes and grain sacks stuffed with be-longings and the necks tied in a knot.

The six-hour run up to Beijing is entertaining. The Chinese are a gregarious lot and soon parcels of food are undone and shared about. A young couple seated opposite us dote over their baby boy. This baby is fascinated by Roselyn and can't take his eyes off of her, but when Roselyn reaches across to touch his hand, he shrieks in ter-ror. This sets everyone round about laughing. Parents and lookers-on quickly assure us in pantomime that they're sorry, but it's just that the baby has never before seen a white person. When everyone sees we can appreciate the humor in this, many come forward to look at us and talk to us. The gathering crowd asks our interpreter if we are *"mei guo ren"* ("American"), and all are pleased when she replies "Yes." Most Chinese like and respect Westerners and to them *mei guo ren* epitomize the West. They are the favorites. The Brits, Germans and French are fine, but Americans are the genuine article. (Of course, the reverse of this coin is that when you do encounter Chinese who loathe Westerners—and there are some—they'll hate the *mei guo ren* most of all. They'll just glare and glare at you.)

Soon three young men join the crowd and establish a monopoly on our time for the next couple of hours. These three young men are clearly a cut above the rest of the crowd. They are very well dressed, have cell-phones clipped to their belts, and they all speak near-fluent English. In deference to these Chinese "yuppies," the young family opposite us vacates their seats and allows the three to sit down. The young men are impressive. All three are in their late twenties, single, and engineers who graduated from North China Electric Power University. They are returning to Beijing from an international industrial exhibition in Zhengzhou where they had been comparing specifications and prices of Phillips, Siemens and Westinghouse turbine generators on behalf of their employer, the State Electricity Board. They are polite, confident, capable, open-minded young men—just the sort of persons who hopefully will help run Chinese society in another generation.

After awhile the conversation drifts towards the Chinese education system, and they explained how all three of them had hoped for non-engineering careers, but had been directed to careers in electrical engineering by the State Education Commission based on their high school examination results. I made the quip that North China Electric Power University didn't sound like much "fun," and asked if any girls at all attended. Oh yes! "We had many very nice, very beautiful girls there." But they added that they did not wish to marry until they were in their thirties and had higher positions, higher pay. They asked about investment earning rates in America. Did I own stocks? They wanted to own stocks.

In time the conversation moved towards politics to the dismay of our "interpreter," Mrs. Jung, a sprightly 60-year-old English professor (and deep-dyed Party member) assigned by our *waiban* to accompany us on our journey. The young men ignore Mrs. Jung's shaking head and ask me about an "incident" in Chinese-American relations that had cropped up a few months previously wherein the FBI had detained a Chinese engineer working at Lawrence-Livermore National Laboratory for stealing U.S. nuclear warhead secrets. The young men query the truth of all this. The Chinese government and Chinese press had denounced the charges as completely bogus, evidence non-existent. Did I believe that the secrets had been stolen?

Yes, I did. There was evidence. The secret data was found inside the accused spy's home computer. Remember you are in no position to judge the truth of such things. You do not have a free press.

The three young men look at me. They don't agree; they don't disagree. They just look at me. The interpreter is not at all happy. She wags her finger in their faces. No more. They desist and drift off slowly. They are not too frightened.

I now take in the scenery.

The line north to Beijing is double-tracked and of a somewhat narrower gauge than either American or Russian trackage—indeed this is the reason behind its original construction: to prevent Russian trains rolling directly south into China in any invasion. Bogeys would have to be changed at the border, forcing a delay. The line is very heavily travelled, with both northbound and southbound trains spaced about five or six minutes apart, and at those time intervals the southbound trains streak past us with a roar and a concussion of air as our combined speeds are exceeding 200 kph. Freight trains and coal trains make up the bulk of the traffic. Out of the east facing windows, Highway 107 parallels us all the way to Beijing. Like most Chinese roads, this highway is tree-lined to provide a protective canopy for those exposed to the elements and travelling by bike, trishaw or tractor—vehicles which far outnumber the trucks, buses and automobiles. The tree trunks are painted white to head height both to deter burrowing insects and to aid night travellers.

Villages, towns, and cities are passed with far more frequency than they would be in America or even Europe, a reflection of the amazing density of population. And in between the settlements are the intensely worked farm fields producing mainly corn and wheat, but also sorghum, beans and all manner of vegetables. Farmers are in the fields hoeing by hand, spreading compost with pitchforks.

Coal is everywhere: heaped beside villages, rail yards, trackside kilns. Smokestacks are the most prominent features on the horizon and contribute to the smog haze omnipresent in both urban and rural areas. The Chinese love of their flag rivals and may even exceed that of Americans, and the red flags are everywhere—atop factory roofs, water towers, construction cranes (where they'll be mounted above the boom tip, counterweight and pivot point), and individual farm buildings. Some farmers even plant the flag in their fields. Another aspect of Chinese life one notices is that despite the heaps of garbage decomposing beside villages, train stations and ditches, there is no graffiti anywhere. It is not a phenomenon that has reached China.

As Beijing is approached the train slows, begins to bump over switches as more and more rail lines feed in toward Beijing West Railway Station. Over twenty tracks are running parallel to each other and the pall of smog grows thicker. The station is approached. If there is a larger train station in the world, I have not seen it. This station, in physical size, is larger than New York's Grand Central, Chicago's Union, London's Euston, Melbourne's Flinder's Street or Paris' Gare du Nord. Beijing West Railway Station's central tower rises over twenty stories, and its mighty wings stretch out to enfold two city blocks.

Indeed, everything in Beijing is built on the grand scale in order to constantly remind residents and visitors that they are in the political and cultural hub of the world's largest nation. And we're not talking here just about the enormity of the Forbidden City and Tiananmen Square which sprawls before it. Nearly everyone in the world has heard of those two unchallengeable sites which were intentionally constructed to physically and emotionally humble individuals, to reduce them to ant-like proportions in the presence of the all-powerful State. No, almost anywhere you go in Beijing you encounter massive man-made structures: boulevards twelve lanes across, apartment complexes that devour scores of acres, and tremendous commercial towers. These towers—soaring, ultra-modern affairs—are not concentrated in a single downtown business district as one is used to finding them in Western cities, but are scattered piecemeal about the vast metropolis. They loom up suddenly out of the ghostly smog that enshrouds the city. They are architecturally identical to the skyscrapers found in any great world city, except for the peculiarity of nearly always being capped with a traditional, steep-sided Oriental tile roof, complete with the characteristic lilting flare at the eaves.

Our accommodation in Beijing, arranged by our *waiban*, is at the Northern Transportation University. This is one of the benefits of being a Western teacher in China—you can travel for next to nothing since all the universities that employ foreign professors must maintain a "Foreign Experts" building or compound to house them and a cooperative scheme has been worked out whereby travelling foreign teachers can lodge at these buildings and compounds for a pittance. This works out to everyone's advantage: the teachers can afford to travel; the *waibans* know where their charges are.

Northern Transportation University has a nice campus—a very nice campus by Chinese standards—and not much below par even by American public university standards. Northern Transportation University is situated in the northwest quadrant of Beijing and is designated as one of China's 100 "Key Universities," that is, one of those universities that is entitled to coopt the nation's top-scoring high school graduates and prepare them for careers in critical sectors of the economy. Northern Transportation University graduates will help design, build and operate the nation's road and rail networks. Although lumping students together in such a narrow academic field and foregoing intellectual diversity might strike Westerners as strange or even unhealthy, the practice does have some real advantages. For one thing, the collective expertise of an entire field of study is always immediately at hand in the form of the resident professors. No need for the professors to be flying off to expensive conferences, since almost everybody who is anybody in their field of expertise is already present on campus. Moreover, the students themselves build up an esprit de corps and close personal bonds at the very beginning of their professional careers. The persons they grow to know on campus will be the same persons whom they will work with the rest of their lives. This, in essence, is the same rationale behind such service academies as West Point, Annapolis and Sandhurst.

The campus has four well-guarded gates at the primary points of the compass that control access from the heavily trafficked city streets beyond. Once inside the campus gates the buzz and honking of the traffic is quickly muffled by the campus foliage. Tree-lined lanes and sidewalks help create an oasis of calm. There is the usual massive statue of Mao facing south and with right hand raised, and sidewalks are lined by glass encased signboards with adages drawn from Marx, Engels, Lenin and Mao exhorting teachers and students to work diligently for the people and earn their privileged position in society. Not bad sentiments really.

The ambience of the campus is perhaps best displayed at dawn when the university's hundreds of retired professors and their spouses (who remain in residence until death), emerge from their apartment blocks for morning exercises. Those in their sixties will be dogtrotting about in packs of four or five, while septuagenarians and octogenarians walk about if they can or, if they can't, simply sit on benches taking the air. These old people are not depressing to look at. Almost all of them still bear aesthetic, intelligent-looking faces with alert eyes. In any campus park or courtyard you care to look into you will see "schools" of these elders performing tai-chi exercises to tape-recorded Chinese classical music. They work slowly but elegantly through their orchestrated exercises: bending, stretching, "pushing hands." Each school's exercises are tailored to the age and the degree of mobility left to its members, who work seriously with inward-looking eyes. Boisterous groups of jogging students always go silent and swerve in a respectfully wide berth whenever they encounter one of these schools of their elders.

In another flowered courtyard a school of "old girls" is engaged in a slow-motion fan dance. Stepping, stepping, balancing on one foot, sometimes a bit unsteadily, opening, closing, waving red fans in unison. They are not without grace. They too work seriously and silently with only a bit of laughing and kidding at the end of each ten-minute routine. What's there to talk about anyway? Most of these people have worked together and lived beside one another all of their adult lives. They know each other, tolerate each other, as well as do old married couples.

We use the week in the capital doing the things foreign teachers in from the provinces usually do: eating at a few good restaurants offering a Western menu, stocking up on books and magazines at the Foreign Language Bookstore in Wangfujing, obtaining items at Beijing's big Friendship Store that are hard to find in the interior, like razor blades, deodorant, cheese, butter (we've brought an ice pack to keep the butter solid until we can get it back home); talking with a few compatriots who you can't help but bump into in Beijing which is ridden with Western diplomats, businessmen, journalists, teachers and tourists whose status is tacitly understood to rank in that order.

Speaking of status, one evening Roselyn and I were seated by our restaurant hostess next to a party of four other *lao wai* (foreigners): three female teachers—an Irish, an Australian and a New Zealander—plus one sensitive-faced Black male who turned out to be a Nigerian medical doctor. This unfortunate gentleman had a sad tale to tell. Although he had graduated from a prestigious British medical college, spoke the King's English and Mandarin, had invested his life's savings into getting to China and setting himself up in general practice, he was failing miserably. He was unable to attract any patients. He would just sit in his office day after day with no doctoring to do. No Chinese would ever come to him, and he had concluded that it was a mistake for any Black to come to China.

He was probably right. The Chinese, despite all the diplomatic courting they do in sub-Sahara Africa, have a deep prejudice against the Black race. This Black doctor would have been wise to have read *Living in China* by China hands Rebecca Weiner, Margaret Murphy and Albert Li. This little gem of a book, a *must* read for anyone contemplating living and working in the People's Republic, clearly warns Blacks of the intense racism they will encounter and advises them to think very seriously about coming to China, a nation whose people will regard them as racial inferiors at best, violence-prone criminals at worst. Rebecca Weiner and her co-authors suggest China's negative stereotyping of Blacks is in large part due to Hollywood's depictions of Blacks, but I am sure the prejudice runs much, much deeper. I can remember the first visit I made to Zhongyue Temple at the foot of Songhan Mountain in Henan. This mountain, the Central Mountain of China's famed Five Holy Mountains, is considered the absolute spiritual center of China, and the first Taoist temple was constructed here during the Qin dynasty (221-207 B.C.). Two of the temple structures, long, narrow buildings that face each other across an intervening courtyard, house hundreds of larger-than-life, painted wooden statues of the multiplicity of Taoist gods. Viewing these amazing, even startling, carvings, each with a visage to represent the virtue or vice they symbolize—for example, wisdom, courage, vanity, and so forth—I noticed only one of the multitude had a black face. Examining it more closely, this fearsome Black god clearly had the negroid features of flared nostrils and large, fleshy lips. Seeing me contemplating the statue, our Chinese guide came over to me and matter-of-factly commented: "This is the Black God. The God of Robbing and Stealing." Then he walked on. Further explanation was apparently not needed.

While in Beijing we also steeled ourselves to take in the usual tourist sights: the Heavenly Temple, Tiananmen Square, the Forbidden City. We loathe crowds and rubbing elbows with camera-toting tour groups wearing color-coded identification tags and being sheepishly herded around by their megaphone–equipped leaders, but we felt compelled by our cultural consciences to make the effort. These premier Beijing sights are, of course, well known to most Westerners through the "Discovery" channel and such movies as the Academy Award winning "The Last Emperor" which was actually filmed within the Forbidden City. These sights are not hyped. They are all they've been cracked up to be. If, anything, a first-time visitor to Tiananmen or the Forbidden City will probably be surprised by just how extensive these two sites are—their size is difficult to convey by means of camera and screen.

We also hired a car and driver for a day trip to the Ming Tombs and the Great Wall. Mrs. Jung came along as our guide. You know, people are funny. By purpose we started for the Wall at first light in order to beat the crowds. As it was, however, hundreds of like-minded tourists must have had the same idea, because hundreds of us were waiting at the Badaling Gate ticket booths by opening time. But what happens once we've paid, and actually mounted the Wall? Ninety percent of us head off east in the same direction. You can see group after group trudge up the stairs to the top of the Wall's walkway and then pause to decide which way to go. The choices are clear. Turn right and scads of people plod eastward like an army of ants; turn left and only a handful of individuals dot the nearly de-serted Wall as far as the eye can see. So what do most people do? They press into the mob and move east. Herd instinct prevails. And, don't get me wrong. We go east too. Mrs. Jung, being Chinese, naturally thinks we should stick with the crowd. "This way better." And against our better judgment, we follow her advice. We push off with the throng.

Everyone has two goals. One is to reach a particular fortress tower of the Wall, visible at a respectable distance, which Mao once remarked was the minimum distance one should walk on the Wall. No man was a "True Man" who turned back before reaching that point. Well, there, at least, is one clear challenge for any self-respecting communist or, for that matter, non-communist. The other goal apparently is to take photographs—lots of photographs—of your progress along the path to "True Manhood." The result is that it's hardly possible to advance through the obstacle course of photographers and photographees. Everyone is either engaged in striking a nice pose or aligning a nice shot. You must pick your way forward carefully to avoid disrupting their work. Meanwhile, professional photographers move in for the kill, plying their trade, taking advantage of the curious, but apparently insatiable, human need to be graphically recorded during key moments of life. Some of the photographers have developed clever gimmicks. One has laid out bows and arrows along the parapet and can photograph you firing arrows down at imaginary barbarian hordes. You can wear an Imperial Chinese soldier's cap while doing so. Elsewhere, at other sections of the Wall, photographic hucksters have set up little establishments just below the Wall. You step over the parapet to their ladder and then climb down to the ground. There they'll have a Bactrian camel corraled. For 25 yuan ($3) you can be hoisted up between the two humps of the surly beast and be photographed with the Wall as a nice backdrop. For a few extra yuan you can choose from a rack of costumes and get yourself up as anything from a Mongol warrior to a Chinese emperor . . . or empress. Don't laugh until you've tried it. This is more fun than you think.

The last two days in Beijing, having gone through almost all of our money, we are forced to spend in our room—Roselyn reading and doing crosswords, me laying in bed watching TV. Chinese television has its own peculiarities. Some channels are state owned, others are privately owned and fund themselves through commercials. The commercials are usually quite good—often clever, very often employing high-tech computer graphics. All channels naturally are stringently controlled. News fare is accordingly absolutely worthless. The Party governs the selection and presentation of every news item. For instance, months after the NATO liberation of Kosovo at a time when even the Serbs were staging mass demonstrations to rid themselves of the accursed Milosevic, Chinese news was still striving to shore that brutal communist dictator up and shamelessly propagating such nonsense as NATO's intervention having caused the mass killing of the Albanians.

A real treat is to watch what passes as a political debate on CCTV-4, the government channel that offers a couple of hours of English broadcasting each day. The host will first pose a loaded question like: "Do the Chinese people living on Taiwan (read: Taiwanese) support the criminal Lee Teng-hui (read: the freely elected President of Taiwan) who wishes to follow the "splitist road" and illegally proclaim Taiwanese independence?" First one political commentator will denounce this as absurd, a total contradiction of the Taiwanese people's eager desire to embrace China and return to the national fold. Then the other partner in the "debate" will say exactly the same thing in slightly different words. And that's it. The host will wrap up the program and these three frauds will turn their slanted eyes toward the camera lens and soberly stare at you.

By far the largest portion of commentary and video footage on any Chinese news broadcast will consist of trumpeting national achievements. If somewhere in the country a ship is launched, a factory opened, a railway completed, the cameras will be there and the television audience will learn a lot of technical information: the weight and maximum revolutions per minute of this ship's propeller, what the chemicals are that are being mixed in this factory vat, what the tensil strength of these steel tracks is.

In a way, I suppose one good thing about Chinese news is that seldom is any individual portrayed in a poor light. Since the news is intentionally upbeat and meant to highlight national achievement, there is little negative coverage. You don't see seamy politicians or corrupt businessmen caught in scandals shielding their faces from the press cameras and ducking into courthouses with their lawyers. No, politicians, professionals, workers, farmers, everyone really, will be dealt with sensitively and shown in the best possible light. The legislator will be depicted bending over documents conscientiously working for the people; the engineer will be seen in hard hat with sleeves rolled up at his construction site; the worker will be earnest and competent as he carries out his task; the poor farmer will be sweating in his field with his back and heart half broken but still somehow manage a goofy, gap-toothed grin for the camera.

The point of all this is of course to show that these people are doing their part too to help build the New China, and that at least is true.

Cultural fare and variety shows are well represented on Chinese television and are usually excellent. The nation has a wealth of talent in all fields of the performing arts and at almost any hour of the broadcasting day viewers can tune in symphonies, ballets or operas. For younger viewers Chinese MTV offers pop music by both Chinese and Western groups but censors out most rap music and the raunchier performers.

Chinese comedies and dramas vary enormously in quality and sophistication since, just as in America and Europe, they must be pitched to an enormous audience within which every degree of intelligence and sophistication is represented. Programming therefore must, and does, range from slap-stick buffoonery and gushy, over–acted soap operas to droll situational comedies and subtle, high-caliber dramatic performances suitable for the most discriminating viewers. With few exceptions, say a long-running docudrama of Mao Zedong's life, one thing most Chinese programs do have in common is that they are low budget by American and European standards. And this is understandable when one recalls that although the Chinese viewing audience is vast, unparalleled, its buying power is quite limited. Commercial sponsors are less likely to be advertising automobiles, investment services, and lawn mowers, and more likely to be advertising a nice bike, a rice cooker, a tasty candy drop.

Now I'm watching a mid-morning dance instruction program. The instructor is a razor-thin, forty-year-old male with a puffy-sleeved pink shirt and black, zipperless slacks that have a top panel that comes way up on his flat stomach and wraps snuggly around him like a cumberbund. His hair is combed straight back pompadour style, and when he turns on his broad, insincere smile, which he does quite often, his slant eyes squint almost completely shut. He is teaching us the cha-cha-cha. His rarely called upon female assistant—a real doll—stands to the side with her hands demurely clasped in front of her watching her boss. You can tell by her eyes that she thinks he's a real jerk—and he kind of is. He's telling us over and over again that it's real important for us to swivel our hips while performing this dance. Each time he tells us this, he demonstrates the proper movement: big hip swivel, big hip swivel.

Even though we've got it cold, he tells us again for the umpteenth time: big hip swivel. But finally he extends his hand towards the girl and she daintily skips across to him. And now they get going, and man you ought to see this guy go. He's cha-cha-chaing all over the place, hips gyrating like crazy, and he just smiles and smiles.

On a very windy Friday afternoon we board our return train at Beijing West. Another flashy double-decker idles on the tracks with conductresses standing at each of the car entrances—smartly dressed girls wearing maroon sashes and berets and China Railways badge insignia. With a smile and a graceful hand motion they invite each passenger to board. We do so, but, being cash short, this time we have to settle for "hard sit."

We get underway and once free of the yard area begin again that rapid electrical surge to speed. As the dusk gathers we're clear of Beijing and back to the sights of the real China. Bare-chested men coated in grey dust as they cast shovelfuls of coal against the wind into trackside brick kilns. Laborers with wicker baskets harnessed to their backs hauling rocks up out of a moonscape of gravel pits. A woman on her hands and knees drawing water from a channel with a scoop on a stick and slinging it on her garden patch. With the wind, half the water is lashed back at her like spindrift. In the fading light, a peasant couple standing on an earthen embankment looking at their field. Their blouses and culottes ripple in the gusts. Each holds a hoe. The man's left hand rests on her shoulder. Chinese Gothic. As the gloom settles, construction cranes now at rest over another of China's numberless factory cities. Red flags stiff in the wind.

A Trip to the Country

It's a fine spring day in April and we have a delicious three-day weekend ahead of us. Eight of us are going to spend it in the countryside. Outside the school's main gate Roselyn and I meet up with the others—mostly graduate teaching assistants from our department. We are all luggageless. No one carries more than a purse or small zip-up handbag as wearing the same clothes for quite a long stretch is not unusual in China. Three days will be nothing. We're a "nice bunch," if I do say so myself. There's Zoe (Wang Yun) who organized the expedition and who seems years older than her actual 23 years. She has the looks and manners of a nun. There's Celia (Yu Yanping), a pert, delightful little thing who wears a smile and a maroon dress with waist straps that tie up in a bow in the small of her back. She also wears thick-soled, clumpy ankle boots to add a couple of inches to her elfen stature. There is Celia's roommate Linda (Wang Erxia), an unusually silent, agreeable girl with a long ponytail and a red and white track suit. She wears white leather flats which are going to leave her tottering about on badly blistered feet before the three days are out. There's Tim (Tian Peng) a married man of 32, rather old for a graduate student, and who has a stocky build. "My wife says I'm a little fat." [Did you catch that? His *wife* says so. He apparently doesn't.] Tim has an unassuming, laid-back

156

manner. He's the kind of man who keeps his hands in his pockets a lot of the time and wears his clothing loose and comfortable. His wife often accuses him of being lazy, but he casually shrugs the criticism off with a smile. Tim's wife, Xiao Li (no English name), is Tim's complementary opposite. She's very active and very attractive, even though she has large protruding teeth and could have profited from orthodontery when she was younger. She laughs a lot, and she talks a lot, and when she talks her hands are forever in motion. She manages a bookstore and Tim. And then there's their daughter: cute-as-can-be, four-year-old Suzie (Tian Xiaoqian). A dewdrop of freshness done up in jeans, shirt, bright yellow jacket and tennis shoes. She has a tiny, up-turned button nose that invites you to look inside and see what's going on in there. She has a yellow hot water flask slung over her shoulder on a strap. She's *ca-ute!* And she's ready to go. She runs to my side and takes my hand: "Let's go, Bill!" Bilingual at four.

We now start our journey. All eight of us wedge ourselves into a 4-passenger bread-loaf taxi which tears off honking and beeping to the train station. But this is a false start. When our northbound train comes in—a battered hard sit/hard stand affair up from Guangzhou, 800 miles and 20 hours in transit so far, it is jampacked with misery. Every seat is occupied, every aisle choked with people, every carriage vestibule brimming with humanity. A scene of unbelievable frenzy now unfolds. Debarking passengers are met and driven back by vastly larger hordes of embarking passengers. Frantic for fear of either not being able to get off the train or not being able to get onto it during its brief five-minute stop, a scrimmage develops at every carriage doorway. Railroad conductors and platform flunkies, faces contorted by rage, rip into the fray, furiously pushing and pulling people this way and that, trying to clear the doorways and lock the doors shut, callously ignoring the pounding on the doors of detraining passengers still trapped aboard. The train begins to slowly glide away. One bold man on the platform suddenly makes an ill-considered lunge for an open window and tries to wriggle his way through, but those inside easily muscle him back out and drop him back onto the platform. Lacking sufficient desperation and athleticism, we eight are naturally left standing on the platform amidst the crowd. We now make our way by foot to the bus station.

At the bus "station," thirty or forty buses of various sizes and stages of delapidation idle in a lot. We board a small one bound for the ancient city of Anyang—the first stop on our journey—two hours to the north. Four of us squeeze onto the undesirable back-seat where the ride is always the roughest, while the rest take what they can get, which isn't much really. The conductor, seeing he's got a full bus, passes down tiny, 8-inch high wooden stools for people to use to sit in the aisle. And then off we go. This might not sound like too much fun, crammed in as we are and being bumped and jostled about, but it is. We're all in high, holiday spirits, chatting, laughing, and passing around fruit and crackers. The bigger the bumps, the more the laughter.

At Anyang, a smog-shrouded, dust-blown industrial city of half a million that once served as China's capital during the Yin Dynasty, we have lunch and then visit the historic grounds. By this time in our stay in China we've visited so many temples and ancient sites that they tend to run together in the mind, and this one only manages to remain memorable by the fact that China's first "divining bones"—actually cattle shoulder blades and tortoise shells—were discovered here back in 1939. These bones and shells bear faint scratch marks that archeologists have identified as being the first known appearance of Chinese character writing. In a glen near the temple is a forest of steles marking the exact location where each of the couple of score of shells and bones was originally unearthed, and a short distance away some rectangular sites have been roped off and more archeological digging is in progress. Heaps of earth are piled around, and in some of the rectangular pits they've dug down 15 or 20 feet. It looks to be slow work with very limited prospects of having any payoff.

After this tour, it's deep into the afternoon, and we need to get going. We hire a van to take us two hours further north and west to Zoe's family home, a farming village at the base of the mountains of the Taihang Shan up near where the three provinces of Henan, Shanxi and Hebei abut. After taking a series of progressively narrower, bumpier and less-traveled roads, at dusk our trip terminates at the end of a dirt road as our van lurches into the age-old brick village of Bai Fu Mang, home to 200 souls. Some of the yokels, and I mean the term kindly, emerge from their walled homes to greet us. Among them are Zoe's family: father, mother and younger brother plus assorted aunts, uncles and cousins. They each have the sun-scorched auburn complexion common to the Chinese peasantry, and offer up hands to shake that are so hard and leathery and with cuticles so coarse and thickened as to seem scarcely human hands at all. Grasping such hands you also instinctively grasp that these are better people than you or I. You just know it. You feel humbled. We are lead into their compound. We are now assuredly in authentic China, seeing the way 70 percent of China's population exists, and it should never be forgotten that China is still first and foremost a rural farming nation.

What are these homes like—these stereotypical homes of rural China? Well, first you come through a heavy, wooden, double-door of fortress-like strength. There is lots of iron hardware to brace and strengthen it. Immediately behind this double-door is a sheltered area where many hundreds of pressed, circular charcoal briquettes, furnace and stove inserts, are stacked eight-feet high, sufficient to meet cooking and heating needs for many months. The focal point of the walled home is the courtyard, a paved-over area fifty feet by fifty feet. This paved area has several small openings from which peach and plum trees protrude. The branches of these trees, now adorned by springtime blossoms, not only beautify the home, but also serve for draping and drying clothes and rags. Also in the courtyard is a charcoal oven reminiscent of an American barbecue pit, and an enormous clay pot for water. This pot is refilled from a cistern located beneath the courtyard. A metal lid like a manhole cover gives access to the cistern. A bucket sits beside the lid. The cistern itself is kept refilled by a complicated system of building rainspouts and drainage grooves molded into the paved courtyard. Plastic wash basins for dishes and clothing are scattered about the court, and another basin, set waist-high atop a wire-frame stand, serves for personal bathing. The stand also has a soap dish and a towel draped from it.

Facing out onto the courtyard are the several small buildings and cells that comprise the home itself. One small cell serves as the kitchen. Like all the other rooms, this one has a floor of bare con-crete. It has a two-burner, gas, table-top stove connected to a gas cylinder. Some old wooden tables and cupboards are for storing the family's woks, pots, bowls and glasses. Various wicker-baskets and plastic containers lining one wall hold eggs, leafy vegetables, peanuts and what have you. A big clay pot holds flour, and there is a table for rolling dough and cutting noodle strips. There are a couple of stools for sitting.

Other rooms facing onto the courtyard store seed and farm implements. Another room has pipes and sheet iron in it. Zoe's father assembles and welds hot water heaters and installs radiator systems in village homes as an important sideline to his farming activities. As it is, most of the farming labor is performed by Zoe's 18-year-old brother, since her 50-year-old father has a serious digestive tract disorder.

A brick cubicle in a courtyard corner houses the squat toilet. This one is kept cleaner than most, but still it is an evil place. If ever there were a device better designed to exact humiliation from its user than the squat toilet, I don't know what it could be. There it is: a six-inch-wide, two-foot-long rectangular slit molded into the concrete floor. An inclined plane tumbles the stuff down and then drops it into a deep pit. Splattering is unavoidable and the stench makes you gag. Spiders and insects commute to and from the pit for dining purposes, and someone has squashed a centipede with his foot. The flattened carcass lies there beside the slit. It is not an attractive carcass. There is a box of shredded newspaper strips and other paper matter to serve as toilet paper. The cubicle also stores some farm tools—mattocks and hoes mainly—and these look nothing like the smooth, straight, finely-turned implements you would purchase in an American hardware store. These are medieval–looking instruments with crooks and bends in the hand-hewn handles.

The largest building of this village home is sited at the northern end of the courtyard and has two stories. As with the other, nearly identical homes in the village, the two-story structure is at the north end of the courtyard in order to shield the rest of the home and the courtyard from the winter wind which blows in from Siberia. The second floor of this structure is used solely for storing the family's crops—in the case of Zoe's family—mainly wheat and corn. The ground floor contains three rooms, two of which are bedrooms, while the third serves as a "living room," although the term doesn't equate well with what Westerners consider a living room as I discovered when first I entered it. For one thing, the floor, once again, is just bare concrete. It had just been doused with a bucket of water and swept clean, but puddles still stood in the floor's depressions. A couch and two chairs are aligned along the wall to the right as you enter from the courtyard. Straight in front of you is an enormous cupboard/dresser combination which stores many of the family's non-perishable possessions: books, papers and documents, clothes, cloths, rice wine, and other odds and ends. Above it hangs a huge plastic "decoration" that is a little difficult to describe. There is a clock built into the upper left-hand corner of the thing with hands frozen at 3:20. The "decoration" itself—and there must be 30 square feet of the thing—depicts a junk sailing across a lake with mountains in the background. The entire scene is done in the most brilliant hues: oranges, pinks, yellows, blues and purples. It is very vivid. In front of this decoration, another one, nearly as arresting, is propped. This second one is a four-foot tall, two-foot wide depiction of Buddha—yellow Buddha, orange background. A well-used incense burner is set at Buddha's feet. Zoe's family are Buddhist, as she informs us, adding enigmatically that most of the wealthier families in their village are also Buddhists.

We sleep that night a deep sleep, a sleep unbroken by any sound in the silent village, and in a bedroom void so dark you can not see your hand held in front of your face. Not a single light burns in the sleeping village—a village in which the generator shuts down at 9:30 p.m. Utter peace.

And we awaken to a dawn of surpassing beauty. We take a dawn walk with the mighty peaks of the Taihang Shan looming over us to our west, the morning sun climbing the sky to our east, smiling down on these terraced fields of the range's foothills. Fields of winter wheat, jade green in their early growth, alternate with other terraced fields of brilliant yellow—mustard plants in blossom. The scene is spectacular. No one cultivates more carefully than the Chinese peasant, and every field is a study in patience and meticulousness. Not a scrap of land is wasted. Every terrace wall is an artwork with rocks so carefully fitted that they needn't be mortared. These walls lean slightly backward to shore up the embankments of soil. Of course this giant's staircase of terraced fields does not allow for any machinery, even if it could be afforded, and there are no tractors in these fields. What there is in the fields are some early-bird peasants wielding their mattocks like picks, bringing then down from the sky, chopping away at weeds ill-mannered enough to have intruded upon the perfect fields. Here and there in the fields are handmade wheelbarrows constructed from bamboo rods and strips. Blossoming peach trees and plum trees splash the landscape with white and pink. An intricate system of tiny irrigation channels brings water to each field and to each step of the terraces. So lovely, and the view seems to go on forever. From the terraced foothills one looks down to the quilt-work fields of the flatlanders below and beyond. And the country roads and earthen footpaths linking the villages of the plain can be traced from afar by the canopies of ancient birch trees that shade each pathway's travellers.

When we return to the village, it is coming to life. It is breakfast time in this village of Bai Fu Mang, and breakfast is the most gregarious time of the day for the villagers. Families emerge from their walled compounds with bowls of noodles or cornmeal gruel in hand and congregate with other families to eat and talk. Nearly all of the 200 inhabitants are visible—standing or squatting in the village lanes, or bunched up in little communal groups on benches strewn beneath the shade trees at the village edge. These folks are very welcoming, friendly and curious of our group. This curiosity is due not only to Zoe's celebrity status when she visits her village— she being the only university graduate her village has ever produced—but also, naturally, to Roselyn's and my presence in the group. None of these people have ever seen a foreigner before. Down every village lane we walk faces appear to greet us, hands are offered up to be shaken, voices echo: *"Ni hao! Ni hao!"* Packs of children race up to us and come to a dead halt ten feet away. Apparently that is what they consider a "safe" distance. Approach them any closer and they fade back; move away and they follow, giggling and smiling. You stop and they stop. You'd like to grab them and tickle them, but they're too quick and wary.

Back at Zoe's family compound we ourselves breakfast on cornmeal gruel, steamed bread, cucumbers and the remnants of a leftover duck. We then board a van—a village "event"—which Zoe has somehow managed to arrange for us, and set off on our day of "fun." The day is rather a blur actually, with stops at several points of interest Zoe has mapped out for us. We visit a Buddhist shrine deep in a mountain cave. We gingerly cross several mountain gorges on swaying footbridges—just weathered wooden slats tied to flimsy parallel cables. Some of these have rope hand-holds, some do not. If they don't, Zoe thinks they're more "fun." The rest of us do not.

Midday finds us at the "Youth Hole" of the Red Flag Canal. This canal, a gigantic irrigation project undertaken during the Cultural Revolution, was hewn by the hands of 100,000 workers over the course of ten years. The single most critical aspect in the canal's construction was the inescapable need to bore a high-elevation tunnel through a mountain spur at a, then, nearly inaccessible reach of the Taihang Shan. To perform this difficult and dangerous work a "Shock Troop" of 300 young fanatics of revolutionary Red Guards volunteered itself. Despite numerous deaths, working in round-the-clock shifts over the course of 18 months, these young men and women hacked a hole through the mountain and freed the waters to pass through. Today the "Youth Hole" is a "must visit" for the region's school children and Young Pioneer groups, and the site can be reached by buses on a precipitous mountain road.

So hordes of kids, and adults too, are at the Youth Hole when we get there. And so also are some reporters. Hardly have we arrived when I get a microphone shoved in my face. Fortunately I've got the interview routine down pat by now in the course of our stay in China, and Tim and Zoe had apprised me of the tunnel's main facts on the roadway up. I'm able to handle the reporters' questions without much difficulty. "Do the people in America know about our Red Flag Canal and our Youth Hole?" "Yes, of course." I lie easily and often in these interviews. After all, I'm here in China hoping to improve relations whenever and however I can, and not otherwise. "Are you impressed with what our young people did here?" "Very impressed. I knew, of course, from the history books that I would be, but I just had to come here to see it for myself—to see it with my own eyes." And so it went.

After this media interlude we climb the upper half of the mountain hulking above the canal tunnel. This takes us a further two or three hours. We wind our way around escarpments on foot-wide ledges, we climb hand-over-hand through narrow fissures using hand-and-footholds cut into the living rock. We cross more swaying footbridges. Finally we reach the peak where a small Buddhist temple perches. Inside there is the usual Buddha, the usual incense burners, and, in this case, off to the side in the shadows, a palm-reading fortune teller. Like all such hucksters who abound in China, this one has gimmicked himself up to look weird. I suppose that's what the clientele demands—working on the assumption that no normal looking person would have been the recipient of such an extravagant talent as the fortune-telling gift. This fraud's costume consists of black pants, black shirt, black jacket, and a grey gangster-style felt fedora straight out of 1920s Chicago. He sports a full facial beard with two extra long hanks trailing down to his chest from the corners of his mouth. He holds a cigar in his hand, but he does not hold this cigar as you or I might, as a normal person would. No, he holds it woven over-under-over-under the four fingers of his right hand. When he draws on this cigar he does so in a wise and thoughtful manner and then exhales the smoke slowly from his nostrils so that his head remains shrouded in a perpetual haze of smoke. His eyes are at once serene and shrewd. If you peek under the little fortune-telling table which sits in front of him, you will see that this worthy is shod in white track shoes. After all, if you think about it, he's got that damn mountain to climb every day.

Roselyn suddenly decides she needs her fortune told. So with Zoe again acting as interpreter, negotiations are opened. We learn that there is nothing so gauche as a single, straight-forward fee. Here you get what you pay for. For a payment of "about" three yuan (36 cents), Roselyn's palm can be read all right, but the fortune foretold would probably not be so good. We are advised by the reader that it would be better to invest "about" five yuan (60 cents)—only two yuan more—and then a much better fortune would almost certainly result. I tell Roselyn by all means to pay the five yuan. The last thing we need at this stage of our lives is a run of bad luck. But before Roselyn can get her purse unzipped, things change. You can tell that the mind behind those shrewd, serene eyes is thinking hard. We are now cooly informed that there is a special, additional five yuan charge for foreigners. This is policy. Roselyn hesitates in mid-zip, and looks at me, but I give her the nod. I've always admired boldness in an individual. Roselyn ponies up the 10 yuan. This ought to be good—and it is. A small crowd is beginning to build as other out-of-breath hikers reach the temple and decide to listen in. This fake, who's almost certainly never laid eyes on a foreigner before—let alone a foreigner's palm—now goes to work. Studying Roselyn's hand he sees immediately that she has a wealthy husband: "You have a wealthy husband." [That's right. I'm the bozo leaning against the pillar who's allowed 10 yuan to be shelled out for this sham.] Furthermore, Roselyn will retain wealth all her life.

[This happy information wins some "oohs" and "aahs" from the admiring crowd.] And better yet, Roselyn, we learn, will have a long life—she will live to be ninety! And, best of all, best of all, she will have many grandsons. No inconvenient granddaughters mind you, we're talking grandsons! [The crowd coos with shared delight.] We're done. We're happy, the crowd's happy, and there is a look of deep satisfaction on the sneakered fortune teller's face. As we go out a line is forming in front of his table and people are fumbling for their wallets and purses.

To get back down the mountain we have to cross one final swaying footbridge to a crag opposite the temple. Here there is a ticket booth—a ticket booth for a monstrous slide—a slide that will skid us down to the Youth Hole from a peak it took us nearly three hours of non-stop climbing to ascend. And the slide ride will last little more than five minutes. That bears thinking about. Our height above the Hole is comparable to that of the Empire State Building. The people down there look like ants—smaller than ants. We're going to descend that distance on a slide that switchbacks down the face of the escarpment and will do so so fast that we're warned to keep yawning to equalize the air pressure in our ears. I lay out five yuan per head for our group and am handed an armload of raggedy, one-size-fits-all shorts in return. Watching weary fellow travellers we see that we are supposed to climb into these shabby, ridiculous looking things to spare our regular pants from being ruined by the slide's friction. Celia, in her maroon dress, deftly steps into her gigantic pair and then bunches her dress up around her waist. The rest of us crawl into ours. We look bad, really, really bad. So stupid. Everyone's joking, sort of. "No pictures!"; "I won't tell anyone about this if you won't."; "This is *so* humiliating." And it is, but it is also quite a bit of fun.

We are now ready to broach the slide entry. Do you remember the feeling you got when you were a small child sitting atop a playground slide and began scooting your bottom towards the precipice? Well, that's the feeling you now get—only magnified several fold. Luckily, however, just before you plummet over you do get help. For each group of two or three people (two or three depending on overall bodyweight) a strong young man is detailed to sit in front of you. He wears an army uniform—not because he's a soldier, he is not, but because an army uniform incites confidence anywhere in China, and confidence is now what you most need. Each of these "soldiers" wears rope-soled canvas shoes—shoes which are badly worn and frayed along their outside edges. You see, your soldier is your "brake." By jamming his feet against the chute's sides he can prevent your momentum from building to unmanageable proportions.

And away we go. First there's Tim, Xiao Li and Suzie behind their soldier, and thirty seconds later there's me and Roselyn behind ours. Zoe, Celia and Linda will follow with theirs shortly. Down and down we rocket. The soldier's soles shriek and smolder to slow us. We whiplash through the switchbacks. Down and down. The ants at the Youth Tunnel grow larger. Now you can make out their individual heads. Down and down. Now you can see their eyes staring up at you, watching you streak along. Down and down. And last of all you can see their smiles. Then WUMP! You shoot off the slide and are dumped seat first into a vat of red plastic balls. Wonderful!

Christians in Xinxiang

No one is sure how many Christians exist in China, an officially atheistic nation, which, although it currently claims to permit religious freedom, simultaneously does all it can to discourage it. It is discouraged in both subtle and not so subtle ways. There is, for instance, a criminal ban on any form of proselytizing, and a prohibition making it illegal for anyone to bring more than one personal copy of a Bible into the country. China refuses to establish diplomatic relations with the Vatican or to allow Roman Catholic priests to operate within the nation. There is a ban on religious schools. Foreigners are expected to keep their religious convictions to themselves. The contract I was obliged to sign states in Section V, Part 4: "Party B shall respect China's religious policy, and shall not conduct religious activities incompatible with the status of a teacher," under penalty of expulsion from China at Party B's own expense. Demanding adherence to atheism as a precondition for Communist Party membership also has an enormous impact since Party membership is an essential prerequisite to gaining appointment to any position of authority in the society, while conversely association with a religion stymies careers and educational opportunities. And there are manifold other harassments and petty nuisances the government inflicts upon the religious in its effort to create a completely God-free society.

Nevertheless, adherents to Buddhism, Taoism, Islam and Christianity do exist in China, and somehow manage to carry on. In Xinxiang many small stores and workshops will openly display small wall-mounted or table top shrines to Buddha with incense burning, and there is a small mosque with Islamic-green domes near the city center. Also there is a non-denominational Christian church in the city, and a smaller (non-Roman) Catholic church. And that's it to serve a city of nearly a million people.

Our first introduction to Chinese-style Christianity came through the services of our dear Nepalese friend, Krishna Singh. (I an revealing his name because he will have permanently departed from China by the time this book is published.) A few days after our arrival in Xinxiang, we were seated at the eight-place table in the "foreign experts" dining room, and, momentarily finding ourselves alone (me, Roselyn and Krishna), Krishna bent over and whispered, "Are you Clistians?" When we nodded, he said, "I too am Clistian." So checking outside the door to make sure no one was coming or within earshot, we softly recited the Lord's Prayer by way of Grace. Afterwards we agreed that we could not risk this behavior except on special occasions and would always be very cautious lest we be over-heard or actually caught in the act by the serving girls, cook, or others who frequently entered the dining room, or by the Party of-ficial who always dined alone in a room adjoining ours.

Later Krishna came back to our apartment with us to talk. He, an advanced computer engineering student who had been at the University three years, warned us that we as residents of the Foreign Compound were carefully watched. I asked him if he thought our rooms were "bugged." He didn't think so, but he had examined his room carefully. I, too, had made a cursory inspection of our apartment soon after arrival. I say "cursory" because as a for-mer naval officer working in communications and cryptography I had on occasion witnessed U.S. Navy and NATO technical experts making security "sweeps" of sensitive communications facilities and well appreciated the utter futility of any amateur detecting so-phisticated listening devices. Moreover, we as foreign teachers and students were such very, very, small potatoes, I couldn't imagine the People's Republic expending a single yuan on "watching" us.

So we spoke openly then and on many other occasions. Krishna had been a Hindu, but had converted to Christianity a year before and had been baptized. He said he was a Catholic, but, as we were later to learn, and to his great surprise, he was not. He also said there was a church he sometimes went to, and we might go there together. I asked if it were a legal or underground church. "Legal. Yes legal." There had been no "trouble" since Christmas when the police moved in to break up the overflow crowd for "public safety" reasons, and Krishna was, as a foreigner, personally taken aside and warned to stay away in the future or he'd be reported to the university authorities. But Krishna never was and never could be a coward, and had attended the church a number of times since his warning. He suggested we go together the very next Sunday, and we agreed.

Bright and early Sunday morning Krishna knocked on the door of our apartment. A short distance from the campus gate we hailed a taxi for the ride across town. Krishna wore black slacks and a black polo shirt to which he now proudly affixed a gold cross. The taxi took thirty minutes to get us through the jammed streets of the city (Sunday being the biggest shopping day in this atheistic land) to the church sited by some long ago missionary in one of the city's poorest quarters. The last block was the most difficult to negotiate since the authorities derive some perverse pleasure in leaving the heavily trafficked east and west approaches to the church unpaved so that worshippers confront an ankle-deep muddy mire through which bikes, trishaws, pedestrians (and our taxi) slew and skid.

Forewarned by phone of our coming by Krishna, a young girl with some limited English is waiting at the church gate to greet us. We are ten minutes late and, to our mortification, the entire service has been delayed on our behalf. Moreover, rather than being allowed to slip in unobtrusively at the rear, we are led down the center aisle of the packed church where three reserved seats await us at the very front. Heads crane to see the strange foreigners. A girl with a camera rushes forward to record the great moment, but desists when Roselyn covers her face with her hands.

Finally, with the three of us appropriately seated, the service could begin. But before I describe the service, let's take in the church setting itself. About 300 poor, unimportant people with mud-spattered shorts, trousers and dress hems are jammed into rows of cheap wooden fold-down chairs. Men sit on the right-hand side, women on the left. Most of the congregation are older folks, probably converted to Christianity by missionaries who operated freely in Henan province and Xinxiang prior to the communist takeover in 1949. But there are some younger people too. The floor is bare cement and, of course, mud crusted. A three-foot high stage is sited at the front of the church, and this has two podiums knocked-up out of plywood set upon it. A large cardboard box with trash and sweepings decorates the left side of the stage. An ancient, free-standing, faded blackboard completely covered in Chinese characters is also upon the stage, while the stage's background is a chintzy red drape with a crucifix affixed to it. Someone has cut foot-long, narrow strips of gold wrapping paper and pinned these in a circle around the crucifix to represent its radiating splendor. A piano sits beside the stage as do twelve middle-aged women in blue cotton gowns—the choir.

With a nod from one of the two older women in shabby street clothes who preside from the two podiums and serve as pastors, the pianist plays and the choir and congregation burst into song—and I mean *burst*. With volume and verve totally unexpected from such a feeble, humble looking crowd they belt out a Chinese rendition of "Onward Christian Soldiers."

There followed a two-hour service of sermonizing, singing and praying. During the praying many of the congregation can be seen to have tears running down their faces so intently do they pray—a sight which moved Roselyn to cry in empathy. The sermonizing to my mind went on far too long and a number of older people were struggling to stay awake. Coughing and hacking were ever present. The old man sitting immediately behind me was constantly grabbing the back of my chair when seized by especially violent coughing spasms and at one point coughed up an immense expectoration and spat it on the cement floor. There was no kneeling, no genuflecting, no crossing and no communion during the ceremony, and I began to seriously question Krishna's assertion that this was a Catholic church.

When the ceremony was over, a nod from the podium started a general exodus, and a number of people rushed down to meet us, or just look at us, including one of the female pastors who motioned with a hand to mouth pantomime that she wanted us to have lunch with her. We begged off, but there was no way we could avoid the multitude of congregationists wishing to touch us, shake our hands, stroke our arms. One old lady with horrible teeth had appropriated Roselyn's left arm and was stroking it like a lap cat.

The scene outside the church was general bedlam as three hundred Christians retrieved their bikes, bundled families, old folks and cripples into the backs of trishaws, and headed for the mud.

Krishna, in the meantime, led us across the church courtyard to a classroom where about 20 youths in their teens and twenties were intently studying a handout sheet printed in Chinese characters and including pictures of the earth, a fish and a clearly Caucasian couple in profile. The young man leading the study group coaxed us on to stools and invited us to watch the lesson progress. It soon became clear that they were studying Creation and the story of Adam and Eve. After ten minutes we decided to leave despite the leader's pleas for us to stay and answer questions. But I said we were not experts, he certainly knew more than us, and we left. But he left his class, followed us into the courtyard and would not desist. He and they had important questions for us. Could he come to our apartment the following night with maybe one other person to get these questions answered? Although very mindful of the warning in my contract, I agreed, but no more than two persons were to come so as to avoid attracting the attention of the officials who oversaw the Compound. They were first to go to Krishna's room, which was under less scrutiny, and then he would bring them quickly and quietly to our apartment after dark.

At exactly 7:30 Roselyn and I and Adam (the American from next door) were waiting in our living room behind closely drawn blinds when we heard a soft knock on the door. Four people were jammed in our foyer: Krishna, a friend of his who was also multilingual and could help translate, the young religious leader and another male member of the youth group. And then they told me there were others. Four Christian girls had pedaled across the city with them, and were at the moment a block away waiting around the corner. Could they come in too? What could you say? They were sent for and told to come quickly and quietly.

Now there are eleven people crowded into our tiny living room. Sitting or crouching around the coffee table, each is poured half a glass of apple juice and offered cookies by Roselyn. It's awkward at first. They mostly just stare at us and smile while we (Roselyn, Adam and I) stare and smile at them. They are fascinated by our blondness, our eyes, the hair on our arms. Time and time again the girls' eyes return to Adam who is not only blond, but young and handsome. We can't lift a glass or cross our legs without our every movement being followed.

Then slowly we begin to get to know one another. Some of the girls know a few words of English, and they ask us to write down our names and then say them. We write and say Bill, and they repeat "Beel"; we write and say Roselyn, and they repeat "Wose-a-win"; we write and say Adam, and they all laugh. They know that name from Sunday's lesson on Creation. The youth leader nods approvingly.

Then we ask them to write and say their names, and this they do with Chinese characters and in the pinyin style using the Roman alphabet. Although I've kept their names, I will not give them here. These young people were aged from 15 to 28 and had at most junior high school or high school educations. All but the fifteen year old were already full-time members of the workforce in factories or low-rung white-collar jobs. Their prospects are not really very good, and I'd be surprised if any of them ever moved from Xinxiang or the province. As such, these young people would be vulnerable if the government ever returned to a policy of active persecution of Christians.

When the kids are not staring at us, their eyes are busy drinking in the "opulence" of our apartment. Roselyn shows them pictures of our grown-up children and our big black cat "Poopy." They do not recognize what the cat is, and at first identify it as a dog.

In time, through the two interpreters, they begin to ask questions concerning religion, and their questions and our probing quickly reveal the depths of their pitiful ignorance.

They didn't know, for instance, whether they were Catholics or Protestants. Asked: "Are you Catholics?," some nod "yes" while others shake their head "no." Asked if they are Protestants, same response. Even their religious leader is not sure. One of the three 18-year-old girls pipes up: "We believe in God!" I tell them I don't believe they can be Catholics because I noticed that they did not take communion in church, did not kneel and did not cross themselves—and I made the sign of the cross to demonstrate. Immediate comprehension! Yes, at the other church in town the people did that! They were the Catholics then! This came as quite a revelation to Krishna who had thought himself a Catholic for the past year.

The religious leader did not own a Bible (which are very hard to come by in China) but pulled out an old, dog-eared, heavily–underlined paperback edition of the Book of John, his main teaching tool. The book was printed in two columns: one column with Chinese characters and the other with the English translation. He asked me to read the English column and confirm that it was a true translation—truly a book of the Bible such as they had in America and other countries. I fetched our family Bible and opened it to John. We set out his copy and mine side by side, and although he could not read English, he could see the letters of each word exactly matched: "In the beginning was the Word, and the Word was with God, and the Word was God." This 28-year-old textile factory worker by day, religious worker by night and weekends, sagged with relief. What he had been teaching was true.

He then asked me about Creation. A question had come up during the Sunday school lesson we had sat in on, and it was one of the questions he wanted to get us to stay and answer. But we had rushed off. The question his students wanted answered was: Were the six days of Creation exactly 24 hours in length like days are today? I told them that some Christians believe so, but that most Christians believe that each of the days are symbolic, representing a stage in Creation that may have taken millions of years. But it is correct to believe either way: 24 hours or millions of years. This seemed to satisfy everyone.

One very earnest young man had a long question that the translator took some time with to get it just right, before he passed it on to me. I was taking notes and these were, I believe, the exact words:

> This man says in China the name for America is "The Beautiful Land" [This is true.] and many Chinese people believes God made America "The Beautiful Land" and made them to be rich and to have everything more than every other peoples because they are the ones that believes in God and go to His church. But now we believes they are having troubles like fires, storms and killings because they stop believing in God and stop going to his church. Is this true?"

I didn't know what to say.

I asked them about their particular church's history, but they knew next to nothing about it. The leader said that all the records had been taken away and destroyed and that only the old ones at the church knew anything. He said the church was built long before the communists came to power. A *shen-fu* (religious man) came and started the church.

"When?," I ask. They don't know, maybe around 1900. "What was his name?" The leader immediately and unhesitatingly writes out three Chinese characters on a sheet of paper, and says they mean something *like* "Malison," but not exactly. I ask if the *shen-fu* was American, but they don't know. All they know is that he was a white man.

The leaders said this man was greatly loved by all the members of their church because he helped the poor, built schools, built clinics and helped parents start businesses—many businesses. He said the *shen-fu* would always be loved for the words he once said and which every member of their church knew by heart.

"Tell the words to me."

> If I had a thousand lives to give—
>   I would give every one to China.
> If I had a thousand pounds to give—
>   I would give every one to China.

Hearing these words, I tell them that I believe their founder was a missionary who came from Great Britain. This is news to them, but it seems to please them. They will tell the others.

I asked the leader why they knew so little about their church and its history. Surely the loss of the written records could have been overcome. But he said the church was closed for many years following the communist takeover and again during the Cultural Revolution (1966–1976). The church was closed and their religious leaders were taken away.

"Did the leaders ever come back?"

"No. They never came back."

"Do you think they were killed?"

"Yes. We think they were killed."

The Chinese girls plead for Adam and Roselyn to sing a hymn. After some coaxing the two very softly sing "Amazing Grace" while the girls, who know it, hum along, and I use hand motions signaling them to keep the noise way down.

The time to go is approaching. The Compound's overseer will

lock the gate at exactly 10:30, and I want the group gone and out of sight by then. One of the young men has brought a camera and we all bunch up for a photograph. Then the four girls say they have a song they've memorized in English and want to sing to us. With their slanted, slit eyes smiling, as well as they can and as softly as they can, and oh so sweetly, they sing:

> In His time, in His time—
> He made all things beautiful—
> Lord please show me everyday—
> As You're teaching me today—
> That You do just what You say—
> In Your time.

Time to go. We say our good-byes inside. Shaking hands, touching one another. We turn off the foyer light and the porch light. The young people crowd into the foyer and wait mute and motionless. I stroll outside. It's raining. I look. I listen. Nothing. Then I motion. They slip out like ghosts and disappear into the night and rain.

Out and About in Xinxiang

Dog Day.

It's Dog Day and I'm going to let the cat out of the bag: dog meat is darn good. Ask anybody in China you care to from poor peasant to Party honcho, lowly waiter to literature professor and you'll get the same answer: it's goo-oo-ood! Some folks will be right up front with you about this. Your waiter, for instance, will be proud to take your order and will give you extra special treatment since he knows he's catering to a true connoisseur. Your Chinese colleague, the professor of literature, conscious of more delicate Western sensibilities, might be a little embarrassed, a little apologetic to admit it and shuffle his feet about a bit, but, if pressed, he too will confess that—gosh darn it all—dog meat *is* good. Absolutely delicious. And it is.

The first time I ate me a dog, and, for some reason, that's the way I always like to put it—"ate me a dog"—I did so with a little prompting from my literary colleague mentioned above. A week or two before, when first we broached the topic and I learned that he was a dog-eater, I guess I must have unconsciously curled my lip, because I could see he was determined to wipe the sneer off my face. He invited me and my wife to dine with him and his wife in two weeks time and on the specified evening he ordered us up a plateful of dog. My wife, a pet-loving type, refused point blank to eat it, and settled on more mundane fare, but I agreed to try it out of a sense of experimentation more than anything. I thought I'd nibble a sliver or two, register the taste in my memory, and then have a good story to tell my friends back home. After all, whenever conversation drifts around to who's eaten weird things, as it seems to do quite frequently in my Texas circle of friends—low brows all—I'd be in solid. A dog-eater can stand tall even among snake, gator and monkey-brain eaters.

But, I must say, what happened at that dining table that night took me completely by surprise. That first bite was like first love. No one could possibly have prepared me for the intensity of the experience. I knew it would be good because everyone had told me so; I just didn't' know it would be that good! After I'd tasted that first morsel, it was like my chopsticks had caught fire. I couldn't poke the stuff in fast enough. I'd no more than get one chunk inserted into my mouth, than I'd be spearing my next. Reflecting back on the experience I feel that I've always known something was missing from my life but I was never able to put my finger on exactly what it was. I recall the innumerable times in my life I've trekked out to the kitchen and poked around in the refrigerator amongst the mayonnaise, pickle and jelly jars looking for something to satisfy a craving, but never finding what I wanted. I'd always come away empty-handed and disappointed. And all along it was dog I needed. That need must lurk deep in the brain, in the hypothalamus most probably—the reptilian portion of the brain, the crocodilian portion.

At any rate having on that night at last found the answer to my craving, I forgot everything else around me: my tablemates, my host, the other dishes, my manners. This was between me and that dog. When finally I got it all polished off and slumped half dazed back into my chair, with my lips and chin all greasy and good, minutes passed before my heart rate and stentorous breathing began to calm. My host, leering at me, gave a cynical chuckle as much as to say, "See, you're no better than the rest of us." And I guess I'm not. Ever since then I think about dog a lot of the time. One of my biggest worries is what I'm going to do to satisfy my unorthodox appetite when I get back to the States. Will I be out after dark scouring my neighborhood for strays? What kind of ugly headline will my local newspaper make of this if I'm caught?

So that was Dog Night, and now it's Dog Day. My wife and I are mounting our Phoenixes and, along with Krishna, pedaling to the outskirts of the city where we've heard a dog market is held each Saturday. We want to check out the scene, learn about this aspect of the trade. When we get there the setting does not appear a wholesome one. At a non-descript village intersection immediately east of the city where the factories are beginning to thin out and farm fields are taking over the dog market is located. While trucks rumble and belch through the intersection, forty or fifty people mill about in a clearing off to the side. The focal point of attention is a row of trishaws and motorized trishaws with cargo boxes mounted over their rear axles. In the boxes—some caged, some quite open— are the dogs.

The dogs appear to be of a very low class. These are not pedigreed dogs; these are not dogs of any specific breed; these are mongrels. Most are medium sized and humble looking. They sit in their boxes disspiritedly with drooping ears and lolling tongues. When you walk past them they duck their heads as though expecting a clout. They don't growl or bark. Some of the mutts have been allowed out of their boxes and are attached to the trishaws by leashes. These pooches snuffle about in the dust to the limits their ropes allow them. They wait for something to happen. They scratch their fleas.

The people who are engaged in this trade—the buyers and sellers—appear to be low-class breeds as well. Apparently the dog trade is a man's business for there is not a single woman present except for Roselyn. Many of these men are shirtless in the hot sun, while others have rolled up their T-shirts to their armpits to expose their bellies and backs to the air. They wear sandals and flip-flops mostly. They drift about studying this mutt or that, meditatively scratching their bellies and crotches. Now and then they'll disengage a foot from a thong and jab their big toe into the loins of a pooch—apparently gauging the thickness of the meat. If satisfied a negotiation will commence, a price eventually settled upon—a high price—not only because dog meat is delicious—a prized delicacy—but because it is the product of a slow-growing animal. This is not a cow or a pig we're talking about—beasts that bulk up amazingly quickly—but an animal that takes many months to acquire a puny 30 or 40 pounds of weight. Dog flesh is *bound* to be expensive. But once the deal is done, the money exchanged, the new owner will lead the scroungy critter away. Man's best friend goes peacefully.

Now I want to eat me a cat.

Opera Night

Relax. You're thinking this piece is going to be about those oft-ridiculed fat people waddling around on a stage, but it isn't. So don't worry.

It's an April evening, Roselyn's birthday, and we're going out with friends to Xinxiang's "Old Beijing Restaurant," probably the most interesting eating establishment in town. The décor and atmosphere have been done up to recreate the Chinese equivalent of *fin de siècle* Europe, that poignantly decadent period which was ushered in by the Boxer Rebellion of 1900 and lingered on until the traumatic convulsions of the 1930s. It was a time of seedy elegance when cigarette-smoking Chinese gangsters in zoot suits could be seen rubbing shoulders with gowned mandarins in the cafes, bars and restaurants in the foreign enclaves of Beijing and Tientsin in the north, and Shanghai and Canton in the south. It was a time, too, when American jazz competed with traditional Chinese music in all the smarter night spots. Such is the "feel" evoked by the rich, dark furniture, the beautiful tiled floors, and the smoky, wainscoted dining rooms of the "Old Beijing."

The stout, middle-aged couple who own the "Old Beijing," forewarned of foreigners coming, greet our party of nine on the restaurant's steps as we disgorge from two bread-loaf taxis. The double-doors are flourishingly opened by two liveried doormen in period costumes: high-collared, gray flannel tunics with matching beanies. Holding with the customs of an older China, these doormen bellow into the establishment: *"Jiu wei, li bian qing!"* ("Nine people arriving. Please come in.") These words are then echoed by waiters and hostesses deeper in the establishment to alert the cooking staff. There is no way you can inconspicuously mince into the "Old Beijing"; your arrival is heralded and reverberates throughout the innermost recesses of the building. We are then conducted with oriental fanfare to our prominently situated table in the main dining hall.

Chinese dining etiquette is much more complicated than it is in the West, particularly in casual, egalitarian America, and complying with its protocol takes practice. I stumble through the procedural minutiae as best I can under Helen's whispered supervision. I direct my *waiban*, Li Qiufa, to take the position of honor at the head of the table, and know to deflect his humble demurrals the requisite three times before I finally get him seated. I then seat his cherubic wife to his right and range the remainder of my guests, four of my graduating senior students (Hou Changwei, Zhang Xin, Yang Hua Jing, Hu Rui-juan), plus Krishna, down the longer sides of the rectangular table. Roselyn and I as the chronological seniors naturally take the far end of the table, to balance the *waiban* and his lady at the other end.

Now I have to deal with the swarm of hostesses, waiters and other attendants who have hastened to our aid. As with virtually every other business and institution in China, the "Old Beijing" is seriously overstaffed. Lots of folk are bustling about. Some are pouring us tea, some are decking us out with napkins, some are issuing us with chopsticks, some are bringing us complimentary cigarettes and lighters, some are igniting the candles on Roselyn's birthday cake, some are fetching us beer, wine and *bai jiu* (the vitriolic 70 proof rice wine used for toasts), and some are focusing lenses on us. Did I mention the fact that no less than five professional photographers and television cameramen are present? No? Well they are. This is an event. A foreigner is turning 52. This, apparently, is news in Xinxiang.

Naturally under the scrutiny of those ruthless lenses there is not a scrap of spontaneity in our actions. We toast, clap and smile, smile, smile like puppets as we work our way through a dozen courses.

The evening's highlight is a recital by a troupe of Beijing Opera performers. Beijing Opera—a peculiar genre of opera—features singers with screeching sopranic voices, fantastical costumes, and absolutely wooden, stylized, set-piece "acting." And although this brand of opera has a certain weird sort of charm, it is definitely not to everyone's taste. Not to mine for one, and I am relieved when it is finally over.

But, to my dismay, as soon as it is over, the owners, photographers and cameramen bustle Roselyn and me out of our chairs to be photographed with the "principals" on stage. Photos and camcorders shoot us with arms draped about these costumed thespians. But then some jerk suggested we put on the costumes. I tried my best to resist, my instinct to preserve my dignity is quite strong, but the hail to put on the costumes was taken up by one and all—the performers, the orchestra, the waiters, and even—blast them—my own students. Before Roselyn and I knew what was happening, we were hustled into the dressing room where a dozen nimble hands stripped us of our outer garments, re-clothed us in Song Dynasty gowns, and propelled us back onto the stage. Applause!

Complete humiliation! Nightmarish it was. And the smirking, sadistic photographers and TV cameramen caught us from every imaginable angle, and in every degrading pose. The prints we managed to recover we now have safely hidden away in a box, but God knows how many others are out there floating around providing fun and laughter to others.

Re-examining these hideous photos one in particular stands out, one I am sure that has provided joy and comfort to my enemies. It's a real gut splitter. There's me caught in quarter profile in my gown (red with big silver dragons embroidered all over it) and wearing my general's headdress: a black beanie that molds onto my head and which has gold tassels that hang to my waist. Now this beanie is not just a plain vanilla one. It mounts upward in red, silver and green stages to form a pyramidical structure, and at its pinnacle sprout two five-foot-long pheasant feathers. When I move my head these feathers slash about in the air. When I stand still, as I do in this photo, the perky pheasant feathers just sort of sprout there. I'm eleven feet tall.

Opposite me in the photo is my wife, and, if possible, she looks even goofier in her gear than I do in mine. Her face is grimmaced up into a huge, rigid smile. You can tell that she's hoping that the audience is laughing *with* her and not at her, but you can also tell she knows that this is a forlorn hope. She's dying. Between the two of us stands Helen, and Helen, because she has had enough sense to stay out of any costume, is smiling quite naturally and appears to be enjoying herself. The photo shows a microphone being held to her face by a TV reporter who's fit to burst. Helen is interpreting for us. There is a series of asinine questions: "How did we enjoy the evening?" I feel so very low, but the reporter can barely contain his glee. "What do we think of Beijing Opera?" The mirthful, malicious

reporter is building to his final question—to the footage you just
know will be clipped for the evening news wrap-up. "How do you
think you look in your costume?"

"I think I must look stupid."

The reporter explodes into laughter.

He doesn't disagree.

Out and About in Xinxiang

The seasons have run their cycle and another summer's come.
Once again, this Saturday morning, as we've done so many times
before, we'll mount those flying Phoenixes for a carefree day of
pedaling around our city—going just wherever our fancy takes us,
doing just whatever we please. Our only plan is to have no plan.
Impulse is everything. As usual Helen and Krishna are with us—our
little family's complete. We're all in jeans and breezy cotton shirts
or blouses.

Krishna takes the initial lead and tools cooly along hunched over
the low bars of his mountain bike. The rest of us follow and have, because of our conventional handle bars, a more straight-backed sitting
up posture. Helen is sitting up straightest of all because her bike's rear
fender is outfitted with a "rat-catcher": a wire box to lock up gro-
ceries, books, jacket or any other valuables she might be toting. The
"rat-catcher" forces Helen forward on her seat and pushes into the
small of her back so that she has to sit up real pert. She pedals knock-
kneed fashion. This might sound a little silly looking, but it isn't. It's
cute looking. Our Helen could never look silly.

We're gliding along in the birch-lined bike lanes, weaving in and
out, flowing with the flow. If Krishna banks left, we bank left; if
Krishna banks right, right behind him we come. Follow the leader is
the name of the game, and we'll take turns playing leader all through
the day. At each major intersection we get jammed up with the
crowd of other cyclists and wait for the white-gloved policeman on
his pedestal to signal us to proceed. Our fellow cyclists smile and
stare at us foreigners—they jabber to each other: *"Lao wai! Lao
wai!"* (Foreigners! Foreigners!) The policeman with the white gloves
stamps his foot, crisply pivots, faces our line of traffic and motions
us to advance. We push off, standing up now on our pedals to build
some momentum, then easing back into our seats. Gliding along.

Half the charm of China lies in the never-ending tableaux of its street scenes—the density of the visual images—the wonderful texture of life here. Dappled by sunlight sneaking through breaks in the birches' canopy, we slip along, entertained by the kaleidoscope of images: the press of pedestrians, the solid chain of sidewalk vendors, the mile after mile of open-faced stores with hardly an arms' span of street frontage. Roll up the shutters and see at a glance the miniscule limits, the single item, that makes up each shop's wares: lamps, bike seat covers, pens, candy, cakes, house slippers, toys, ropes and cords, pots and pans, women's underpants, stools, teas, plastic wash basins, bicycle tires, wedding dresses, funeral wreaths, nails, brooms, bicycle pedals.

Sights that once would have arrested me no longer do. My eyes still see, but the sights, all of them, slide by smoothly now with never a rasp or catch, all of them just part of the seamless pageant. We pass a 70-year-old man with shaved head and naked to the waist harnessed to a coal cart that must weigh a ton. The sinews in the man's neck and back are strained taut. The bones of his ribcage are there to be counted by anyone who cares to do so. We roll on by. A man makes his way along the sidewalk. He has a primitive wood-and-hide drum tucked under his arm upon which be beats out a tattoo. He wears a rope belt to which a dozen dead rats have been tied by their tails to form a skirt. He's a professional rat-catcher. This is a business. We roll on by. A middle-aged man in a tattered blue suit sits on a curb with a plastic wash basin between his feet. A half dozen goldfish swim in the basin. This is a business. A woman has run a long cord out of her second-floor apartment window. She sits on a stool beside a little table with her red telephone upon it. Need to make a call? This, too, is a business.

We take our lunch at a sidewalk noodle shop and find ourselves in People's Park in the afternoon. Biking down one path we come upon the camel ride. For 10 yuan ($1.20) a man gives you a short ride on his camel plus a Polaroid shot of yourself enjoying the ride. When we happen upon the scene three unattractive teenage girls are arguing that 10 yuan should do for the three of them if they all ride together: one ride; one photograph. The camel man grumbles but eventually gives in. The three girls climb up a step ladder and wedge themselves between the two humps. This beast, like all the brethren of his species, has a crummy personality, and snarls and lows once he takes their weight. The camel has a wooden dowel piercing his septum, and it's only by jerking viciously on a rope attached to this dowel that the camel can be made to move even a few steps. That's the ride. The camel stops. The man snaps a photo while the three girls offer up coquettish smiles and whatever minimal charms they have. They then dismount and eagerly bunch up to see the instantly-developed photograph. Their smiles fade. They don't like what they see in the photograph. They refuse to pay their 10 yuan. An argument erupts. The camel man is furious. He yells; he stamps his feet; he waves the photograph in their faces: "This is how you look." A crowd gathers and the onlookers begin to join in. The photo is snatched from the camel man's hand and passed around. The crowd thinks the camel man should give the girls another ride and try for a better shot. The camel man, shaking his head in despair, caves in. The girls prepare to remount. We pedal on.

At the center of People's Park where the various lanes and paths converge are a handful of sad little carnival rides and nearby some small vendors have set up snack and drink stalls. Here, beneath a gaily colored umbrella, we sit to refresh ourselves and to "people watch" as young couples, families and old folks stroll by. To our left is one of those lovely, arched, oriental-style footbridges, and up and over it come two elderly women: one of whom is merely old; the other of whom is ancient. They may be mother and daughter, or, this being China, perhaps more likely, mother and daughter-in-law. At any rate, they proceed with great difficulty. The ancient one, clinging to her companion, teeters along on the tiniest of feet, bound feet, wincing with every step. When they reach our snack area, the ancient one very slowly and carefully lowers herself into a chair. Once seated she uses her hands to lift each of her legs in turn and to position them just so. Each foot is no more than five inches long, and the arch of the foot comes down so abruptly from the ankle that the overall effect is reminiscent of a horse's hoof. Each foot is shod in a black cloth slipper with a strap across the top which looks like something you'd find littering a nursery floor. The woman sits with her hands on her knees and studies her feet.

Time passes, and now, cresting the arch of the bridge, comes a wedding party—a peasant wedding party—in from the country. The dozen or so men and women of this party have the form and color of baked bricks: unmistakably field people, unmistakably poor.

Bottle-brush hair and severely Asian faces. They come on tentatively like soldiers foraging in a strange, possibly enemy, land. They're bunched together and trying to look inconspicuous though this is difficult because of the bride: a gauzy white ball of fluff at their center which they appear to be guarding. The group advances towards the carnival area, then halts and huddles up to confer on tactics. An older male detaches himself from the group and approaches the proprietor of an idle merry-go-round. Money changes hands and the wedding couple are coaxed forward. A lever is thrown and the ride is started. A tape recorder begins to play the tune of 'Pop goes the Weasel." The ride is small and uncomplicated. A handful of carved wooden horses, camels and zebras fixed on poles revolve on a small platform. The poles do not go up and down. The couple, seated on two of the animals, hold hands and go round and around. At each revolution they laugh and wave to their waiting group.

At the conclusion of this enjoyment, the group proceeds to an ice cream stand, and the same older male as before, who behaves as though he is the bride's father, hurries forward to pay out money. Cones of various flavors are passed about and the wedding party stand licking their cones, catching drips with their tongues. They keep to themselves. Occasionally the bridal couple glance self-consciously about, but they avoid meeting any bystanders' eyes. When the cones end, so does the reception. Flanked by the other members of their group, the couple moves off, bearing whatever modest dreams they might have. They retreat back over the bridge from whence they came.

The Ferris Wheel

We bike over to the ferris wheel. This is really the only true "ride" that the People's Park offers—the only ride that matters. It sits—towers—off on its own amidst a vast expanse of concrete. It's a little daunting as you approach it and especially when you stand at its base and look up at it. It's way up there. It doesn't move at all quickly. In fact, its movement is barely perceptible. But if you look closely you see that it revolves like the hand of a giant clock, making one complete cycle in thirty minutes. Your ticket is only good for one go round. Because it moves so slowly, the ferris wheel never stops. There is plenty of time for the attendant to disembark riders and embark others without ever having to stop the revolving wheel.

Okay, it's our turn. The four of us slip inside our gondola which has a wire mesh cage enclosing it. We're off! We settle ourselves in and sit facing each other on two benches. The gondola's car slowly, slowly begins its ascent. After a time we can begin to see People's Park spreading out below us. It's quite beautiful. Lanes wind here, there and everywhere, and upon them all kinds of people stroll. On the artificial lake, families and lovers labor cheerfully away in paddle boats going nowhere in particular but leaving momentary wakes on the pond's placid waters.

In our cage everyone is smiling. We can see other people in their cages and they're smiling too. As we rise higher and higher our horizons expand and we can see beyond the park: the city now begins to spread out below us, growing larger and larger and larger with each passing moment. Our "kids," Helen and Krishna, are exhilarated. Helen begins to sing—no words—just a beautiful da-da-da-da-dee-da tune in that heart-stoppingly pure soprano voice of hers. Krishna is full of beans too and is standing up in the cage, moving about. He puts an eye up against the wire mesh so that he can see out with an unobstructed view: *"Wo de tian! Wo de tian!"* ["Oh my God! Oh my God!"]

Fifteen minutes into the ride and we approach the apogee. Breathtaking! We can now see all of the city—home to nearly a million people—and into the surrounding area beyond: the farmlands and farm villages, the artificial fish ponds which ring the city and help to feed it, and the billowing chimneys of the huge and numerous concrete-making plants on the city's grimey western fringe. Here, midway through our ride, we are fully exposed and our gondola is buffeted by heavy winds. Everything shakes and rattles. Helen, ever cheerful, laughs and giggles. Krishna: *"Wo de tian!"* Roselyn and I just sit and smile. This, too, shall pass. We're happy.

And then, of course, we begin the inevitable slow descent. For some reason, looking out upon the scene, seeing the homes of a million people, but a scene ever-shrinking now, I'm reminded of an incident that occurred more than thirty years ago. It was when I was in the navy, back in the Sixties, and on an aircraft carrier. We were in the far north Atlantic, sliding through a pitch-black night with "darkened ship" in force. Greenland was somewhere out there off our starboard side. And on this quiet night, in the wee hours of the mid-watch, one of the sailors in our Communication Center set a number of teletypewriters to work in tandem printing periods— just dots—all through the night. By the morning he had run off yards and yards and yards of paper printed with these dots. He had printed out one million of them. And he then taped up these million dots all over the Communication Center's walls. When we, the members of the morning watch, came on duty, he announced to us with great amazement in his voice: "Look. That's one million. That's what a million looks like." It was overpowering. Simply overpowering. We all just looked and looked. I know all of us were thinking the same thing: we humans, we are just that small, just as insignificant as one of those million dots—even more insignificant: the earth has *billions* of people. You know, in a vague sort of way, it was kind of comforting. There was a message there if you cared to read it: relax—don't take your life so seriously. You're not going to change the world; no one person is. The pressure's not on you.

So now, that's what I'm thinking. This city has a million people, and here we sit in our cage. Just four little dots. But what lovely dots I'm with for now—people whom I love so dearly that it actually hurts. And down and down we descend. Mellow now I am. How I wish this ride would never end. But it must. At any moment now the attendant will be opening the door. And we must exit.

Leaving

Our last few months in China were played out against a back-drop increasingly somber in tone. Much of this sadness had to do with Helen's situation. Despite all our efforts we were unable to se-cure for her a visa to continue her studies in the States. Even though we had splendid cooperation from the administrators at my home institution, the University of Texas at Brownsville, who swiftly sent Helen a letter of Acceptance and aided Roselyn and me in setting up an America-China Friendship Scholarship which would have covered all of Helen's schooling and living expenses for up to three years while she pursued a Masters in English, and even though my good friend Mark Wiggins, an officer in London's Ovum Corporation and a previous manager of its Asia-Pacific operations, had promised to try and place Helen in one of the corporation's China offices once Helen had her Masters, the U.S. Embassy Visa Unit in Beijing twice rejected Helen's application. Why? Who could possibly object to this girl's coming to America for three years of study? I'm not sure I'll ever know the answer. My faxed query to the Visa Unit, with characteristic rudeness, was never replied to. When my congressman, Solomon Ortiz of Texas, pur-sued the question on my behalf, the U.S. Consul in Beijing in-formed him that it was because Helen (1) had no credible workplans upon her return to China, and (2) had no previous experience of international travel. This was an astounding reply, Helen of course did have definite work plans, and as for having no record of previous international travel, one wonders what planet the consul has been living on. What possible opportunity would a 22-year-old girl from impoverished central China have for travelling abroad? Does he think she could have gone on overseas holiday jaunts with her family? Does he think she could have flown to Cancun for Springbreak?

Very possibly so, because I don't think our foreign officers in China have much knowledge of China or the Chinese other than what they happen to pick up from Chinese political and business types they might encounter at cocktail parties in Beijing. I don't think they have much feel for ordinary Chinese citizens—probably regard them as riff-raff. No, if you want to see what our U.S. representatives in China look like, go to the big, four-story "Friendship Store" complex a couple of blocks from the American Embassy. There you will see our well-nourished embassy and consular officers come swaggering over from their exclusive, gated, foreigners-only apartment blocks to relax at Starbucks, enjoy a calorie-rich luncheon at Pizza Hut, spoon down a nut-sundae at Baskin-Robbins, and pick through the coolers at the Western-style supermarket for their cocktail party hors d'oeuvres. You see, this is the tiny, artificial world their lives revolve in; this is the "China" they know. The only real Chinese people whom they get to know are the poor wretches who are handed a number and herded into the visa-hearing rooms. With their supplicants before them and safe behind their inch-thick, bullet-proof plate glass our consular officers then get to exercise God-like authority in making or breaking lives. And, oh my, how they revel in that power. My son, who used to work in Panama, said he sometimes drank at the bar where the Marine guards of the Panama City legation congregated. He said the marines—none of whom could be accused of being overly sensitive—often spoke of being sickened by how the visa officers laughed and joked about jerking this or that visa applicant around, and made bets on who could make the most applicants cry in a day.

Well, I hope the visa officers and the U.S. Consul in Beijing are proud. They really did a job on our Helen—and on Roselyn and me too. The three of us had built up such beautiful dreams around her coming. She would fly home with us, sitting between us. We'd all hold hands when we took off. Our empty home would come alive with her laughter. She could move into our daughter Kirstin's old room. She'd have her own bathroom and shower. She could go and come to the university with me until she learned to drive a car of her own. Roselyn planned shopping expeditions with her to get, what Helen refers to as, "the fashionable clothes." Helen was looking forward to cooking for the three of us in the evening, serving us Chinese meals her mother had taught her. We'd use chopsticks. Then there would be three Christmases with the whole family decorating the tree together. And when the three good years were up, our son and Mark Wiggins would be sure to place Helen in a suitable job back in China.

The thought that all this happiness has been thrown away because some soulless visa officer got up on the wrong side of the bed or, worse, had a $10-bet with the others to see how many Chinks they could reduce to tears that day really, disturbs me. And it very well may be true.

I'm not going to continue with this rancour. I know it isn't pleasant to read about, and, anyway, most all of us have experienced similar frustrations in our lives—running smack up against a bureaucratic wall of stupid indifference—a wall impervious to compassion or even common sense.

The end result for us, in human terms, was twice seeing our Helen spat out from the Embassy Visa Unit gate with her slanted eyes awash in tears. Then there were the two long train rides back to Xinxiang with Helen slumped against Roselyn's shoulder. What sadness. Helen's life in China, with the prestige of a master's degree earned in America behind her, could have been so much better, so much easier, than it now is going to be.

To make matters even worse, in the final months of our stay, Helen was beginning to pay a price for her close association with us. The fact that she had the luxury of spending her afternoons and evenings in our heated/air-conditioned apartment, had the use of our private toilet and shower, made some people jealous. So, too, did the clothes we sometimes bought her. Helen didn't have many clothes and the clothes she did have were not "the fashionable clothes," but hand-me-downs from her two older sisters. We bought her a pair of new shoes, a white blouse and a black suit so she'd look her best for her Visa hearings. We bought her a $20 watch to replace the clock face of a man's watch (her brother's) which she always carried in her pocket. But, perhaps, what most excited others' envy of Helen was the frequent leaves of absence she was granted in order to serve as our guide and interpreter on trips. These trips took her to many of the cities of China—a rare opportunity for any Chinese. Roselyn and I on a number of occasions asked Helen if her association with us was causing her any problems, but she always said no—no problems. But I wasn't so sure.

And, naturally, the shoe eventually dropped. It was in May. Roselyn and Helen had gone up to Beijing to meet our son Russell who was flying into China on a one-week business trip. (We have a great photo of the occasion: Helen beaming and holding up a big sign, "Welcome to China, Russell" as my son comes towards her.) The following night, Roselyn, Russell and Helen were due back in Xinxiang on the 9:40 evening train. That same afternoon Spring (Wang Yixuan), a friend and classmate of Helen's, came to see me, wondering exactly when Helen would get in. There was to be a Party meeting that night, and Helen was on the agenda to be the fifth and last of five people who were to be "discussed." I knew what this meant: Helen was going to be publicly "criticized." Soon after Spring left, two of Helen's closest friends, Jennifer (Hou Changwei) and Jane (Yang Hua Jing), came to see me, stressing how important it was to get Helen to the meeting room by 10:00 p.m. If the meeting had to be held up beyond 10:00 on Helen's account, it would not make things any easier for her. I asked Jane how bad it was going to be. Jane thought a moment or two before replying: "Maybe not so bad." That gave me no comfort at all.

Krishna and I were at the station with a waiting bread-loaf taxi when the 9:40 train rolled in. We bundled Roselyn, Russell and Helen into the taxi as quickly as we could, and tore off for the university. As soon as we had gotten into the taxi I laid my hand on Helen's back and said: "Listen to me Helen. There's a Party meeting in progress at this moment in Number One Building. The meeting is being held in session until 10:00 and your arrival." She understood everything in a flash. With my hand on her back I felt her breath catch and her whole body tense. Her hand shot to her mouth. "I'm going to be criticized," she gasped. That sounds melodramatic, but there is no other word for it. She "gasped." As the taxi

whipped along, Krishna calling for greater speed, Helen was thinking as fast as she could. Her eyes stared straight ahead: seeing nothing; picturing everything. She knew what was going to happen.
Forty Communist Party members—students and faculty—were
waiting for her. First she'd be asked to confess all her shortcomings
to them, then afterwards they'd each get a crack at her.

The taxi made the Number One Building with three minutes
to spare, and she leapt out of the cab and ran up the stairs. I was
proud of her: she wasn't crying.

Of course she was crying—sobbing—thirty minutes later
when our apartment door flew open and she made her way unsteadily towards the bathroom, one hand covering her face, one
hand feeling the way before her. Roselyn went after her, and moments later Jane and Jennifer came running to the apartment. They
were shaking their heads: "It was so vicious, so cruel."

The "highlight" of that criticism—I guess you could call it
that—came when the chief antagonist, a vituperative, fortyish faculty member, went to work on Helen. While she sat on a bench beneath a Chinese flag and a Deng Xiaoping portrait, he lambasted
her again and again. Never once deigning to use her name, instead
referring to her as "somebody," he bullied away at her, trying to
break her spirit, "Somebody thinks her class can't get along without
her. Somebody thinks she's too good for the others. Somebody has
become haughty. Somebody has become too busy to bother herself
with her classmates. Somebody thinks about herself and forgets the
community. Somebody has become an individualist and forgotten
she is a communist." And on and on.

But even though there were such ugly scenes as this in those final
months, I don't want to give the impression that there were no good
moments. It wasn't just a case of one dreary day following another.
There were still some cheery days; for instance, the days of our king-
size son's visit. Russell, always exuberant and easy going, kept everyone about him laughing during his stay. He even came along with me
to class, talked to the kids about nothing much at all really, and thoroughly charmed everyone. At our apartment in the evenings students
would gather about his chair like he were some jolly Buddha and laugh
and banter with him. "Russell, you are so strong!" That's the Chinese
face-saving way of saying, "Russell, you are so fat."

Another nice time came in June with the graduating seniors'

talent show—the Senior Concert. Judges held auditions and whittled the performances down to the sixteen best. One of these was a squaredance which Roselyn and Mr. Lu would lead. The eight girls in the group would wear white blouses and full, floor-length calico skirts, while the eight guys were got up in white shirts, jeans and floppy farmer's hats—the closest thing to cowboy hats that they could find in Xinxiang. For two weeks the group practiced at least two hours per day. They were good; Roselyn was good. Gay, lively and charming.

Indisputably though, the real star of the evening was to be our Helen, the dancing champion of Xinxiang City, who had also won many prizes for her singing. Four of the sixteen performances would feature her, and the evening's program had to be built around her so that she would have time to change costumes and catch her

breath between her appearances. Helen's mother and second elder sister (herself a dancing and singing instructor) came down from Jiao Zuo to stay with us for the night and to share our prime seats in the 2,500 seat auditorium which was filled to overflowing. I saw Helen half an hour before the show began at a time when already the aisles of the auditorium were choked by the "standing room only" crowd. She was still in her street clothes, but her stage makeup had already been applied: her face was caked in white powder and her features had been drawn on extra large. Seeing her close up was a little disconcerting. I asked her if she were nervous. She laughed. "Why would I be nervous? This is my forte." "Forte" was a recent addition to her vocabulary and she'd been using it a lot in recent days. And there was no question that she understood its meaning. Her performances were stunning.

First was a Tibetan folk dance for which she had chosen and trained six other girls. When the curtain came up they were arranged on the stage in a triangle like bowling pens with Helen at the apex, closest to the audience. The girls wore white satin gowns which had sleeves six feet long that would emphasize their arm movements, while the girls' long braids were held tightly to their backs by being tucked beneath their belts—so their sleeves would swirl and their hair would not. They all wore headdresses and had gold coins dangling from gold chains strung across their foreheads. They danced with haunting sinuousness to Li Na's "Stepping into Tibet." Helen's grace was matchless, and as she danced she wore her brightest smile and her eyes were on her mother and sister and me—letting us know that, while she might be pleasing others, she was mainly trying to please us.

A couple of acts later and it was Roselyn and Mr. Lu on stage with their troupe of sixteen square dancers. This dance went down very well with the audience—it was listed in the program as "Roselyn's Dance"—and had the whole audience clapping in rhythm. When it was over Krishna and I went on stage to present Roselyn with a bouquet of carnations each. The Chinese like such gestures, and the applause grew even greater as we came off the stage.

Then it was the star's turn again. The curtain went up to reveal Helen standing alone, floodlit in a brilliant cone of red light, gowned, too, in communist red. She then sang "Red Bean," an old Revolutionary favorite about parting loved ones and parting comrades. She sang in Chinese in a voice so pure and poignant that many of the audience were moved to tears. As the song drew to a close I moved to the side stage steps, and just as it ended I came forward and, with two hands, presented to Helen a bouquet of red carnations. What I had intended to say as I gave her the flowers was, "Beautiful, Helen," but somewhere I lost the comma and it came out as, "Beautiful Helen." I didn't realize her microphone was still on. There was another mighty applause.

Helen's third performance did not start off well in my view. The curtain went up to reveal six dancers spaced about the stage with Helen at the back. I had an immediate jolt of disappointment. What's she doing way at the back? She's the dancing queen; she should be up front! I didn't want to be wasting my time looking at these other people. But I soon caught on. The dance was modern disco style with the tempo racheted up at set intervals. With each increase in tempo a progressively better dancer came to the fore to display his or her dancing skills, each display requiring more athleticism, more talent than the one before. Finally, when the last stage in the musical tempo was reached and the beat was going so fast that you could not imagine any human being possibly being able to keep pace with it, Helen rocketed to the front and, for what must have been two solid minutes, put on an electrifying display of her dancing talents: incredible athleticism, incredible energy. Every part of her body was in a fever of movement, but each image of her body that the eye was quick enough to catch in that blur of motion was alight with that unfailing grace of hers—a sheer pleasure to the eye. A roar of applause accompanied Helen throughout the final minute of her performance.

Two more acts and then came the finale, and when the curtain went up I could see right away that this time everything was in satisfactory order. One-hundred-and-thirty singers were in five tiered ranks to form a choir—all dressed in white, all anonymous. To the front, off to the side, one person dressed in blue: Helen. One person holding a microphone: Helen. She would sing in counterpoise to the 130 singers of the choir. Two songs were sung; one in Chinese, one in English, and in each Helen's voice, pure, sweet and glorious, suffused the auditorium. Lovely finish.

Two other happenings which lifted our spirits during those otherwise sad final months were Helen's securing of a job and her trip. One of the repercussions of Helen's being refused a visa to study in the States was that it left her high and dry as far as her future was concerned. One reward Helen had earned for being ranked first academically in the English department was automatic acceptance into Henan Normal University's Graduate School. Unfortunately, when she decided to pursue the visa, this reward was taken away from her and given to the second-ranked student. By the time we learned of Helen's second rejection by the U.S. visa officers in Beijing, Helen's opportunity to go to Graduate School had been lost. So now she had to find a job. Thankfully, one of Helen's female professors had a contact with a joint venture company in Zhongshan, and here a position was found for her. The company produced copper tubing and, while the management and factory workers were Chinese, most of the engineers were Brits and Americans. Helen would serve as an interpreter/translator go-between, and although the pay was not high (about U.S. $120 per month), Roselyn and I would pay her a monthly allowance to insure her life would not be one of just bare subsistence. She would share an apartment with two other of the company's female employees. Helen was content with her prospects—and, of course, she would persist in her efforts of obtaining a student visa for, in her words, ten years if necessary.

But before Helen would start work in mid-July she had her trip to take. As a weak sort of compensation for her not getting to go with us to the States, Roselyn and I decided to give Helen a trip to Southeast Asia as a graduation present. This greatly excited her. Originally we planned for her to accompany us for a month in Malaysia and Tioman Island but this ultimately proved impossible. The authorities would only allow her to travel with other Chinese as part of an organized tour group that would collect in Shenzhen and then visit Hong Kong, Thailand, Singapore, Malaysia and Macau. As it was, even this trip caused us enormous hassles to arrange thanks once again to the callousness and arrogance of the U.S. visa officers in Beijing. Presumably they didn't think they had hurt her badly enough in just rejecting her visa application, they had to rub salt in her wounds by stamping rejection notices into her passport—something that was totally unnecessary for them to do and so damaging to Helen. It made the authorities in all other countries reluctant to admit Helen even as a visitor. They'd ask themselves why do the U.S. authorities keep rejecting this person and re-fuse to allow her into their country? Do they know something about her that we don't? Is she a prostitute perhaps? At the same time, the rejection stamps caused the Chinese officials to suspect Helen of being a defection risk. Just one day before Helen's trip was set to start, a Chinese foreign affairs officer screening the tour members' passports saw the rejection stamps and decided he wouldn't allow Helen to go. This would have been another mighty disappointment to Helen but for the magnificent efforts of our *waiban*, Mr. Li, who had worked very closely with Helen and us during the long, failed campaign to get her the U.S. student visa and who had come to share our disgust and disdain for U.S. visa offi-cers. He was determined not to let them harm her any more than they had already done with their needless, arrogant rejection stamps. He managed to get the Chinese foreign affairs officer to re-verse his decision. She would be allowed to go if her family would put up a 10,000 yuan surety bond against her defection. The money was put up. Also Mr. Li got the police in Xinxiang to certify that Helen was of good character and not a prostitute. With only an hour to spare before a taxi was to take her to the airport, the last stamps and certifications were secured. She would go after all.

Helen's quickly packing for her trip, all sweaty from running around town with Mr. Li and Roselyn getting the permits and cer-tificates. She's wearing the dress she's picked for her first ever flight in an airplane—a frilly white thing with big purple flowers printed upon it, and fluffy gauze petticoats beneath that cause the dress to flare out like a bell. It's like something a ten-year-old American girl would have worn to a birthday party back in the Fifties. Helen looks very young; she looks very sweet; she looks like a doll. The new carry-on bag we got her lies open on our living room floor, and Helen squats before it Chinese style, sitting on her heels, and starts folding clothes and packing. She scuttles about crab-like in her squatting position. Her brow is scrunched up in a thinking frown: "I'll take this yellow blouse. I think I'll leave these shoes. I'll take these two pairs of socks. I'll take this little purse." Zip, zip. It's done. She's packed. We go. Roselyn, Krishna and Helen's mother will take her to the airport in a taxi and see her safely off in the plane. But I have classes to teach. A quick walk to the school gate; a quick hug; me waving to a disappearing taxi.

A week later at 5 o'clock in the morning Roselyn and I made that same journey to the airport. We were leaving China. The week had been a painful one of farewell dinners and visits by our students and other friends. Our apartment was continuously filled with students who came to be photographed with us, to give us cards and gifts, to say good-bye. The monitors of each of the seven classes I taught also dropped off class gifts: memory books that each student had written in; a taped recording in which each student spoke a message to Roselyn and I; class photographs. With these photographs, these written and spoken words, we should be able to recall each student forever. How these students have touched us. Quite truthfully, I did not want to leave these students, to leave Xinxiang, to leave China. Is what we're going back to better? No. Will we be happier? No. Will I somewhere find students as good and decent as these? Never.

Postscript

Tioman Island, Malaysia-July, 2000

I'm floating. Once more Roselyn is on the beach talking with Dave—"Tiger Man." Dave never did find that gold tooth and so has a big black gap where the tooth should have been, but he's adjusted. Now whenever he smokes he just grins and plugs a cigarette in the hole. There have been a few changes at the cottages, but not many. This year's monsoon sent twelve-foot waves crashing ashore which washed away a shack and a few palm trees, but there are still plenty of trees left. Most of "the boys" have gone too—drifted back to the mainland or, in one case, gotten into trouble with drugs and had to be let go. But otherwise things are pretty much the same.

My routine here is soft and easy. I sit on the cottage porch and write from dawn's light till noon when I knock off work for the day. I lunch with Roselyn at the Chinese restaurant just a short stroll down the beach, then nap, float for a while, and at dusk have a few Tigers with Dave, Roselyn, and the human flotsam which tends to wash up at the cottages.

Right now it's my floating time. I float; I think; I remember. I'm remembering last week when I took the ferry to the mainland and bussed up to Kuala Lumpur to see Helen. Her tour group had reached Malaysia, and would be in K.L. for a day. She had gained the permission of the tour guide and Party member accompanying the

199

group to leave the group and be with me from seven in the morning to eleven at night. Of course they took basic precautions to prevent her defecting: holding her passport, keeping her suitcase and possessions, requiring her to phone in her whereabouts at set interval during the day.

I picked up Helen at her hotel room—she roomed alone because her roommate had defected three days previously when the group reached Singapore—and we had a golden day together. For the outing Helen had chosen a sari and matching top of a startling bright green hue with big yellow flowers. "Do you think my clothes are too bright? I think they might be too bright, but I bought this dress and top in Thailand and haven't worn them yet."

"No, they're not too bright."

We spent the day walking, talking and shopping together. Shopping for souvenirs for her friends and family and herself. Trifles really: postcards, a key chain saying "Malaysia" on it, a two dollar pair of earrings, a box of coconut candy. She even had a surprise gift for me—a flashy black belt with a white diamond design on its back and a metal buckle in the shape of a stingray. "Do you like it?"

"Yes, I do."

For supper I took her to a Western-style restaurant near the Central Market. That's what she wanted, something Western, something modern, something new and different to her. The place was small, atmospheric with its table candles and mood music, and no more pretentious than these places usually are. It catered almost exclusively to an Anglo-Saxon clientele. Helen liked it.

When the waiter came I told Helen to order whatever she liked, and she did. Coming into the restaurant she had seen the dessert tray near the door and remarked that "those sweet foods" looked good, and so asked to see the foods on that tray. The waiter looked at me, I nodded, and the waiter went to fetch the tray and explained to Helen what each dessert was. Helen selected the mango pudding. The waiter asked Helen if she wanted to eat the pudding now or later, and I put in that we Westerners often ate our dessert at the end of a meal, but Helen said she'd like to eat "the sweet food" first and so she did. She then followed her dessert with a plate, or rather a platter, of rice and then a plate of shrimp. She ate the rice and shrimp as two separate courses: first the rice platter, then the shrimp. Her dining utensil was the serving spoon that came with the rice platter. Roselyn and I had taught her how to use a knife and fork some time before, but she ignored those two utensils. "I don't know why you foreigners have the knife and fork. The spoon can do all the jobs." She scooped up a shrimp and started crunching it. Helen eats shrimps entire: heads, eyes, antennae, tails, shells, everything, the same way she does crabs, although the crabs are somewhat noisier to crunch and pulverize before she swallows them. But the shrimp are pretty noisy too, and while Helen masticated away at them she sat with her elbows on the table dangling her serving spoon and happily studied her fellow diners. Some of her fellow diners studied her too.

I delivered Helen back to her room a few minutes before her eleven o'clock curfew and, thanks to the defected roommate, had a little time alone with Helen before leaving. She curled up on the couch beside me, laid her head in my lap, and I petted her. I stroked her cheeks. "How did you get such smooth skin?"

"All girls—all Chinese girls—have smooth skin."

I trace the outline of her eyebrows with my finger. Her eyes are closed and she smiles, and now I'm gently running my fingertip down the stiff little bristles that form her eye lashes. "Yes, but how did you get such beautiful eyes?"

"I don't have beautiful eyes." She tugs at one of her eyelids. "These things are too fat and thick. They make my eyes bulge out."

"Yes, but how did you get these cute little ears?" I'm tracing the curlicues of her ear folds.

"They're not *cute* little ears." She giggles and slaps the couch twice: slap, slap. "They're just ears."

After a bit more of this nonsense, I borrowed her trip diary and took a taxi back to my hotel. When I was back in my hotel room and had crawled into bed, I opened the diary and started to read: "June 23, 2000. Morning. This is the first day of my trip. I'm now waiting in the Waiting Hall No. 5 waiting for my flight. How shall I describe my feeling now? Exciting, nervous or frightened? Well, I don't know. Mom worries about me a lot. I saw her crying outside the gate. She still regards me as an unfledgling bird, not knowing to deal with anything. This trip is a big test to me. I'll prove her that I'm already a big girl and that I'm able to experience and deal with all kinds of things by myself. June 23, 2000. Night. The room I'm staying in is nice and cool. Lying on the bed I try to recall what has been happening through the long day. The excitement of getting on the plane, the relief I felt when I saw the nice man waiting to pick me up after getting off the plane and the spectacular scene of Shenzhen. So far, so good. I'd better go to bed now. Another exciting day is waving at me!"

I read the diary through to the end, then turned out the light. Perfect daughter. Perfect day.

At 8:00 in the morning I was back in her room, helping her to get ready for her departure. Her group would leave for the airport just after nine for the flight back to China. I didn't want an awkward airport good-bye with scads of strangers standing around, so there was just this one final hour to be with Helen, and most of that time was consumed in exchanging information: be sure to get me your address and telephone number when you start your job in Zhongshan; mail these letters for me once you're back in China; remember these are the steps you will need to go through if you want to try again for a U.S. visa. "I won't stop trying. Not if it takes ten years. I won't stop trying. I won't despair."

And before we knew it, the time had flown away. Only minutes to go now. A long, long hug with soft words spoken, soft words shared.

I then asked Helen if I could listen to her heart. "How? Where?" I led her to the bed and she laid herself out like a patient with her arms at her sides. I knelt beside the bed and rested my head on her breast. She took hold of one of my hands while I listened. What a sound. BOOM-boom . . . . . BOOM-boom . . . . . BOOM-boom, or perhaps it was HEL-en . . . . .HEL-en . . . . . HEL-en.

I asked her not to move, just to lie there. I stood up. I looked at her one last time. She looked at me. Those glycerine almond eyes. Daughter of mine; daughter of China.

So now I'm floating. Lapped by the waves; sun full in my face. My eyes are closed and I'm listening to a beating heart.

It is beating now, deep in the heart of China.